WHAT ARE WE WAITING FOR?

What Are We Waiting For?

Finding Meaning in Advent & Christmas

Richard Leonard, SJ

Paulist Press
New York / Mahwah, NJ

Cover image [to come]
Cover design by Sharyn Banks
Book design by Lynn Else

Copyright © 2014 by Richard Leonard, SJ

Library of Congress Cataloging-in-Publication Data:

Leonard, Richard, 1963–
     What are we waiting for? : finding meaning in Advent & Christmas / Richard Leonard, SJ.
        pages cm
     ISBN 978-0-8091-4906-3 (alk. paper) — ISBN 978-1-58768-449-4
     1. Advent—Meditations. 2. Christmas—Meditations. 3. Catholic Church—Prayers and devotions. I. Title.
     BV40.L47 2014
     242'.33—dc23

                                                                        2014018737

ISBN 978-0-8091-4906-3 (paperback)
ISBN 978-1-58768-449-4 (e-book)

Published by Paulist Press
997 MacArthur Boulevard
Mahwah, New Jersey 07430

www.paulistpress.com

Printed and bound in the
United States of America

To Frank Leonard, Ray O'Leary, Maurice Duffy,
Trina Cambourne, Ray Crowley, Tom Cruise,
Des Dwyer, Michael Hill, Margaret Laffin,
Andy Hamilton, and Bill Barry:
companions and guides who waited with me.

CONTENTS

PREFACE

I have always found the season of Advent an odd time, in the sense that some people speak and act as though we are going through it for the very first time, that we don't know how this story will end. It's the same in Lent and Holy Week where some believers have very long, sad faces as though they have to pretend they have never heard about Easter.

Christian celebrations are all about *anamnesis*, a Greek word meaning "to recall" or "to remember." However, in the life of the Church and especially in our liturgies, this remembering is not passive. We do not just recall the events of our salvation: the birth, life, death, and resurrection of Jesus; we enter into them, repossess them, allow them to repossess us, and enact them again. This sacred drama, acted out for us and upon us by God, calls for our full, active, conscious participation as well. And it's because we know how this story ends that we give ourselves more wholly over to it every year, because *anamnesis* is about a repetition that gets deeper and richer every time.

This is why the title of this book is, in a sense, asking the wrong question. Maybe it should have been, "Who are we waiting for?" "What" usually implies an event, whereas "who" always refers to a person. But in Advent it is always both. What are we waiting for? We are waiting for an event who is also a person: Jesus Christ the Lord.

The word *advenire* in Latin means both "to come to something," and "to arrive somewhere." One meaning is about a journey or an approach—an anticipation; the other is a completion, a joy, or possible relief, at journey's end. There is something cyclical here, which is just right. Until we die, or until the end of time, there is no completion to the pilgrimage of faith, just new approaches and fresh beginnings. So the person/event we are waiting for is here and now, and is also yet to come, a great tension that draws restless hearts on to Christ who is the journey and the destination.

Christianity is the only world religion to believe that God, the Creator of the universe, took flesh of our flesh, bone of our bone. It's an extraordinary claim, isn't it? But we hold it passionately and proudly because it votes such confidence in humanity, giving us such dignity. It also reveals how our God works—in the created order, in and through the ways of the world, and, most especially, through the crown of all creation, humanity itself.

Rather than follow through the three-year cycle of readings for the seasons of Advent and Christmas, we shall initially explore the two major themes that emerge in any and every Advent: preparing to celebrate the birth of Jesus, and preparing to receive Christ at the end of time. Later we will reflect on Christmas; the Holy Family; Mary, the Mother of God; the Epiphany; and the Baptism of the Lord.

ACKNOWLEDGMENTS

I would like to thank:

Mark-David Janus, CSP, Paul McMahon, and the team at Paulist Press for their continuing belief in me and my work, and for enabling me to talk to a very wide audience about faith and life;

Steve Curtin, SJ, and the Australian Province of the Society of Jesus for the education and formation I have received, and their ongoing support to do the "greatest good for the greatest number";

Fr. Brian Lucas and the Australian Catholic Bishops Conference who understand that the communication's ministry involves various forms of the presentation of the Word;

The forebearence of my Jesuit community at North Sydney, whose support and care, at home and while away, provides a home base for a ministry often lived "with one foot in the air";

My mother, Joan, who taught me how to tell a story—and showed me the impact it can have.

1

PREPARING TO CELEBRATE CHRISTMAS

Expecting the Unexpected

*A*t the start of Advent 1992, I was appointed to the parish within the red-light district of Sydney and promptly refounded the church choir. The first chorister to apply was a very tall, beautifully dressed woman who approached me after Mass and said in her *basso profundo*, "Father, my name's Gloria and I sing bass." "It's always hard to find basses," I said. "See you tomorrow night for our first rehearsal." As Gloria walked off she stopped, turned, and said, "You realize I'm a trannie don't ya Father?" "Yes Gloria, even I had figured that one out— it's unusual to find a woman who can actually sing bass."

Gloria was, without question, the worst bass I have ever heard in my life, but word about her spread like wild-fire in Kings Cross, and soon many of her friends were coming to Mass to see and hear her sing. One Sunday, at the end of a hymn, Gloria let go of a big "AHH-MEN" and soon there were two pews of transvestites on their feet yelling out, "You show 'em girl."

I know it will come as a terrible shock to you to find out that not everyone in the Catholic community was coping! Indeed a small group started a petition asking us to immediately remove Gloria from the choir, because "she was making a mockery of the Mass and is a distraction to our prayer."

Eventually, the issue came before the parish council. Just as they were about to vote on whether Gloria should be asked to leave the choir, my Irish-born Jesuit parish priest spoke up. "You know," he said, "Jesus was always strong on 'reading the signs.' In Advent, we are always being called to 'read the signs.' Maybe, just maybe, Gloria is a sign to us this Advent that God's gifts do not always come to us in little neat boxes. In fact, you know, in chapter 14 of Luke's Gospel, Jesus talks about signs and says that 'when you give a banquet go out and invite the poor, the crippled, the blind and the lame.' Now, if you ask that fellow, confused as he may be, to leave the choir we may never see him or his friends again. And last I checked I thought the sacraments were for those who most need them. You don't have to get your act together to get God in the sacraments. You have to get the sacraments to get God. Maybe Gloria is a 'sign' to us this Advent that God comes to afflict the comfortable, and comfort the afflicted." "But," he concluded, "I could be wrong, so go ahead, go ahead and have your vote." We won the vote! Gloria remained.

After six months, Gloria told me that her wife was dying of cancer in another city, and that she needed help to face up to her issues and return home. While undergoing counseling, she vanished from the parish. Then, one day, a man turned up on my doorstep. I did not know who it was until he spoke. "G'day Father. It's Gordon and I've just come to say goodbye."

A good while later a letter arrived from Gordon, who wrote requesting that we read it out at the Sunday Masses. "I just want you to know that last night at home my wife died peacefully of the breast cancer she's had for the last eighteen months. After the undertakers took her away and I put our boys back to bed, I was overwhelmed to think I wouldn't have been here if it wasn't for the goodness of the parish at Kings Cross. I know it wasn't easy for some of you having a drag queen in the choir, but you believed in me even when I didn't know who I was, what I wanted, and where I needed to go. Who could have thought that singing at Mass was eventually going to play itself out into reconciling a husband to a wife, who was such a model of forgiveness, and giving back to two boys their dad, because they've done nothing to deserve to be orphans? I'm not sure if you're aware how often you sing of and preach about 'amazing grace.' Never stop doing that. I am a witness to its power. And if I understand it correctly, amazing grace says it doesn't matter where you start; it matters where God's love can finish it."

> Amazing grace! How sweet the sound
> That saved a wretch like me.
> I once was lost, but now am found,
> Was blind but now I see.[*]

---

[*] The text by English poet and Anglican clergyman John Newton (1725–1807) was first published in 1779.

Grace is just a fancy theological term for God's saving love. It is what our preparation for Christmas is all about. May this Advent enable us to realize afresh that the signs of God rarely arrive in little neat boxes, and that, through amazing grace, we should expect the unexpected by journey's end.

Keeping Our Eyes Open

These days most people keep vigils because they are anxious. We wait in hospital corridors for news of a sick relative. A parent stays up with an infant who may be teething or has a high temperature. We might even sit by the phone waiting to be reassured that a loved one is safe and well, or that we have passed the exam, been accepted into a course or college, or we got the job. Many of these occasions can be highly stressful vigils.

Some people keep vigils that are filled with excited anticipation, as when some young adults sleep out to get tickets to a sports game or a concert, or when we see the old year out and the new year in.

It was not long ago, however, that vigils were a much more common feature of people's lives. There were vigils with the dead. There used to be all-night vigils of prayer, especially when parishes had perpetual adoration of the Blessed Sacrament. Some still do. Perhaps before any of us can remember, there were also vigils kept with the bride the night before her wedding, when she waited and watched for the sign of her approaching groom and his attendants. The Church has enshrined the experience of keeping vigil through the Vigil Mass on Saturday night, the Vigil Ceremony in the funeral rites, and the most important one, the Easter Vigil.

Whatever the vigil might be about, it is almost always a very good indicator of what or who we truly value. And the discomfort of "vigiling" is discounted by the end result.

Advent is like one, elongated vigil in preparation for Christmas. In this regard it is like Lent, and that's not by accident. Through the first millennium of Christianity, Advent was a later Lent. Both were five weeks long, marked by fasting and penance, and both gave the faithful a day off halfway through. Advent, however, got shortened to four weeks in the tenth century, and Pope St. Gregory the Great eased the fasting and penitential aspects of this season in the twelfth century. He knew that preparing for Christmas should not be primarily marked by being anxious about sin, but by being filled with a growing sense of joy.

This is so much so that, in every Advent season, we have Gaudete Sunday, literally the "rejoicing Sunday," and it used to mirror Lent's Laudate Sunday, that day of respite halfway through our fasting and penance. Since the tenth century, our rejoicing day is not so halfway anymore, but that's no matter.

All Christians should take joy very seriously. We all know that the Gospels never record Jesus as laughing, but as James Martin, SJ, capably demonstrates in *Between Heaven and Mirth: Why Joy, Humor, and Laughter Are at the Heart of the Spiritual Life*, some of the parables in their cultural context would have been hilarious. This sense of humor can be lost on us.

Pope Francis knows that in any season, and even when it is out of season, joy should mark our Christian lives. "The Christian message is called the 'Gospel,' that is, 'the good news,' an announcement of joy for all people; the Church is not a refuge for sad people, the Church is a house of joy." On another occasion, the Holy Father said, "If we keep this joy to ourselves it will make us sick in the end, our hearts will grow old and wrinkled and our faces will no longer transmit that great joy—only nostalgia and melancholy, which is not healthy....[They]...have more in common with pickled peppers than the joy of having a beautiful life." He called his first apostolic exhortation *The Joy of the Gospel.*

Taking the pope's words to heart, let me give you one piece of advice this Advent: If you are a happy Christian, can you please tell your face about it sometime soon? Catholics, especially, can be the gloomiest lot you ever want to see. Sometimes before Mass begins in my parish at North Sydney, I encourage the congregation to greet all of those around them, especially any visitors we may have. Usually the front half of the church warmly indulges me. The back half can look at me contemptuously with a glare that says, "I don't do that nonsense, get on with it—you have forty-five minutes until I'm out of here."

In Australia we have seen some fine young Catholics drift to evangelical churches. While the reasons for this drift are many and varied, every time I have been to a Pentecostal community, I have been generously and explicitly welcomed. The congregation seemed to be genuinely joyful to be there. I always compare and contrast that experience with what I see and encounter in some of our own churches.

Our lack of joy, of course, can be a symptom of serious spiritual illnesses. It can sometimes show how a believer thinks they have to earn God's salvation or that they have to save the world or that they can never be worthy of God's mercy and love. None of these are laughing matters. They are heresies. Only God saves us through unmerited grace. Though we cooperate in salvation, it is the Trinity who affects salvation for the world. And there is not a person who is beyond the mercy and love of God.

The sort of joy I am advocating here is not walking around with a supercilious smile on one's face, pretending we do not have a care in the world. That's a pathology. Christian joy is about knowing where we have come from, why we are here, and where we are going. That should put a spring in our step.

Our preparation for Christmas is a vigil of growing joy at what God has done for us in Jesus Christ, and it should work against anything that might see us end up pickled peppers!

Waiting in Line

I think we should pluck up our courage and just come out and say it: all colonial powers are oppressive forces that are particularly destructive of the local indigenous people and their culture. That said, of all the European colonial powers we might have had, I thank God we had the British. I think the USA, Canada, and New Zealand might be grateful too.

Apart from the glories of the English language, if the British had a colony for long enough, it left behind five institutions: parliamentary democracy; a generally incorrupt and competent civil or public service; the rule of law; the best education, healthcare, and welfare it had at the time; and, most importantly of all, a military who takes orders from the elected government. For all the British Empire's many and manifest sins, all these claims cannot be made of any other European colonial power.

However, one of their finest cultural legacies is also one of the most overlooked: the ability to queue, or wait in line. If ever you have been overseas, you know that the Brits do it best of all, followed by the countries they colonized. Though other European countries have offered the world priceless other cultural gifts, the joy of patiently waiting in line is not one of them.

In a train station at Paris years ago, I remember standing in a very long line for a taxi. I had never seen jostling, shoving, and abuse like it in my life. And when "Madame," holding her miniature dog in her arms like it was a baby, pushed in at the front of the line, all hell broke loose. The Italians and Spanish hardly know what a line is, and the German and Dutch do it well enough, but rather humorlessly.

The native English-speaking world, however, is very good at lines and waiting to be served. It is even better when the line throws up a much-appreciated, and until that moment undiscovered, comedian. One-liners abound, and a star is born!

The success of waiting in line entirely depends on patience, knowing that everything is going as efficiently as possible, and that we will soon be rewarded for our time and effort.

One of the biggest themes of Advent is to cultivate patience. We are given many readings where John the Baptist and the prophets encourage their followers to be patient, for the age of the Messiah will soon dawn. The Israelites needed to be patient. Each generation hoped and prayed that they would be the one to witness the appearance of God's anointed. The Jews still hope and pray for this to happen.

The Christ, however, did not come as many expected. Some thought he would arrive with a flourish and in a dramatic event. Others argued that his arrival would usher in the end of the world. Still more said it would be a regal entrance that would see the political overthrow of the Romans.

The very people who longed to see the Messiah missed out because they became impatient, or they were convinced it could only happen one way—their way.

John the Baptist is the first to publicly see Jesus for who he really is. He recognizes that Jesus' sacrificial love can fill our valleys, lay mountains low, make crooked paths straight and rough ways smooth.

Advent is the season of the "patient yes."

Every year all of us in the church figuratively stand in line and remind ourselves of how blessed we are to have seen our salvation in Jesus. It was worth the wait.

We remember the faith of those who longed to see what we see and to know what we know. And we cultivate our patience for life's valleys, mountains, and crooked paths where sometimes we can feel Jesus' absence more than his presence, where it is only when we look back that we can see that he was with us as we went uphill and down dale.

The virtue of patience also means we get a handle on our place in God's creation. Seneca the Younger, the great Greek philosopher of the first century AD, observed that those who had the most money and thought themselves the most important were the ones who seemed to get most angry—about everything. Think about what happens at an airport when a storm hits and, through no fault of the airline, the plane gets canceled. Who makes the most noise? The first class passengers! They think their money and position will inoculate them from things going wrong, from waiting patiently in line. It sometimes does, but never all the time. Who makes the least complaint? The one for whom this trip was a gift, and their seat was right at the back, next to the restrooms.

Advent keeps us humble, knowing that we are the direct beneficiaries of God's patience with us, and that, through no time and effort of our own, we have been definitively rewarded.

As we wait together in line during Advent, let's do so with good humor and keep saying yes to all that salvation holds for us: yes to God's personal love, yes to Jesus' kingdom of justice and peace, yes to every opportunity to serve the gospel, and yes to knowing that our God is a companion with us at every step of our journey.

The Key of David

I love the great Advent hymn, "O come, O come, Emmanuel." The origins of the text are disputed. They come from a hymn, "Veni, veni Emmanuel," which is either from the eighth or twelfth century. The origin of the music is not disputed. It was written in 1850 by John Mason Neale, a priest of the Church of England. He came across the text that year, translated it, and adapted a fifteenth-century French Franciscan chant to suit the text. In English, this hymn has become an Advent favorite.

> O come, O come, Emmanuel,
> and ransom captive Israel
> that mourns in lonely exile here
> until the Son of God appear.
> Rejoice! Rejoice! Emmanuel
> shall come to thee, O Israel!*

Advent is all about announcing that "God is with us." However, sometimes that can all be a bit too otherworldly, that the Emmanuel we are singing about is only about God visiting us from on high. That's true, but it is equally true that God is with us from within.

The Doll and a White Rose, attributed to V. A. Bailey, is a moving story that reminds us that the ways God comes to us sets us free from the things that ransom us, and those ways can be very unpredictable.

---

* "O come, O come, Emmanuel" is the mid-nineteenth-century translation by John Mason Neale and Henry Sloane Coffin of the ecclesiastical Latin text "Veni, veni, Emmanuel."

I hurried into the shop to grab some last minute Christmas gifts. I looked at all the people and grumbled to myself. I would be in here forever. I hurried to the toy department and wondered if the grandkids would even play with my gifts.

At the counter, my eye caught a little boy holding a doll next to me. He kept touching her hair and he held her so gently. I watched him turn and ask, "Aunty Jane, are you sure I don't have enough money?" Gently, the woman replied, "Emily doesn't need a doll, David." The woman went to another aisle.

The boy continued to hold the doll. David looked so sad that I couldn't resist asking who the doll was for. "My sister wanted it so badly for Christmas." I told him that maybe Santa was going to bring it. He said, "No, Santa can't go where my sister is....I have to give the doll to Mommy to take to her." I asked him where his sister was. He looked at me with tear-filled eyes. "She has gone to be with Jesus and Daddy says that Mommy may have to go be with both of them soon too." My heart nearly stopped beating.

David went on, "I told Daddy to make sure Mommy goes nowhere until I got back from the store. I want Mommy to take this doll to Emily."

While he wasn't looking, I reached into my purse and pulled out some cash. "David how about we count that money again?" He grew excited. "I asked Jesus to give me enough money. I just know I have enough." I slipped my money in with his and we began to count it. He looked up from the count and exclaimed, "Jesus has given me enough money for Emily's doll."

In a few minutes his aunty came back and I wheeled my cart away. I could not keep from thinking about the little boy as I finished my shopping in a totally different spirit from when I had started.

On the way home, I remembered a story in the newspaper several days earlier about a drunk driver hitting a car and killing a little girl and that the mother was left on life support. Two days before Christmas, I read in the paper where the family had turned the machine off. The day before Christmas there was a funeral notice saying that a Requiem Mass would be celebrated on St Stephen's Day for Julia Norris and her daughter Emily. Michael was their husband and father, and their son and brother was David.

As I gathered with my family in front of an overblown meal, which none of us could finish, holding expensive gifts we didn't need, and drinking more alcohol than was necessary, I thought, "We've lost the plot with Christmas." God-with-us arrives as a simple child in need of love, and in the honor of that day, we spend too much money, eat too much food, and get drunk.

I left the table, went to my desk, and wrote a card for each member of my family. I told them what I'd never been able to say before: "I want you to know I love you."

When they read those cards, my family thought I was losing it, but through David and that doll, God visited me in the last week of Advent, and Christmas will never be the same again.[*]

O come, Thou Key of David, come
and open wide our heav'nly home;
make safe the way that leads on high
that we no more have cause to sigh.
Rejoice! Rejoice! Emmanuel
shall come to thee, O Israel!

A Complex Birth

Before I became a Jesuit, I was a diocesan seminarian, and during the Christmas holidays, I worked in the pastoral care department of a big Catholic public hospital. At a Christmas party, I met the charge nurse of the maternity ward. Pleading that because I was a celibate I would never be at a birth, I inquired if I might be allowed to "come and see." The charge nurse thought that would be fine. Six weeks later I got the call. Apparently a student priest watching a person have a baby is not an easy sell! But Mary was sixteen, had been dumped by her nineteen-year-old boyfriend, and shunned by her family. A kindly seminarian was better than no one at all.

---

* Adapted from "The Doll and a White Rose" by V. A. Bailey. Source unknown.

On arrival at the maternity ward, I did antenatal class 101 in ten minutes. All sorts of commands were barked at me:

- hold Mary's hand;
- when the midwife tells Mary to "push and keep it coming, keep it coming, keep it coming"— you say it too;
- don't get in the way;
- and don't faint!

Mary and I met six hours into her labor, which was an unusual circumstance within which to meet your "birthing partner." She had very little small talk, maybe because she had no breath at all. From my vast experience of child birth, I thought everything was going along swimmingly until the doctor arrived to perform an *episiotomy*. If you don't know what that is, you don't want to, and I wish I never did. I swear before God that analgesia would have been invented centuries earlier if men had to go through all of this. We would go on epidurals in the sixth month.

The baby arrived minutes later. Mary wept. She had very good cause to weep. I wept for no good reason, and the charge nurse wept because I was weeping. There is something so primal and human about the moment of birth that it bonds us to each other. Friendship born in the trenches took on a new meaning for me.

After the tears, came the laughter and joy. The reality of Mary's tough situation was happily postponed.

On discharge, Mary asked me to baptize the baby. I couldn't. I was a long way from being ordained a deacon.

I arranged for a priest friend to do it and became Benjamin Michael's godfather. I have stayed in touch with them for the last thirty years. Mary went on to have three more boys to three different fathers. Tommy, the last dad, is now her devoted husband.

When he was four, I got Benjamin into the local Catholic primary school, where the principal was Sr. Mary Francis Xavier. She was formidable but fair. She took an interest in Benny and his brothers. She was able to arrange for a scholarship for each of them. Sister only had to go to Mary's home once to demand that the boys got out of bed, were fed, cleaned, dressed, taken to school on time, and later did their homework. It paid off.

Benjamin was a good student and Sr. Francis Xavier despaired that Mary would be sending him to the local high school. It had a terrible reputation. On behalf of the boys, Sister applied for scholarships to a Christian Brothers High School. On their own merits, Benny, and his brothers in turn, won a place. Sister wins a place in heaven. Benny is a physiotherapist, Daniel is an accountant, Kai is a social worker, and Noah is a nurse. He has just finished obstetrics.

Mary works at the local supermarket. Twenty years ago I received her and Tommy into the Catholic Church and married them in the eyes of God. She now volunteers at the St. Vincent de Paul's local hostel for homeless women. Some of them are sixteen years old and pregnant.

From a complex conception, a messy birth, a willing midwife, and a vulnerable baby, extraordinary goodness has flowed from one generation to the next. The divine working through human hands at every stage has changed lives. For us preparing for Christmas, this story comes as no surprise. Rev. John Bell of the Iona Community tells us why:

> Light looked down and saw darkness.
> "I will go there," said light.
> Peace looked down and saw war.
> "I will go there," said peace.
> Love looked down and saw hatred.
> "I will go there," said love.
>
> So he,
> the Lord of Light,
> the Prince of Peace,
> the King of Love,
> came down and crept in beside us.*

I love that phrase: "Came down and crept in beside us." No fanfare. No palace. No earthly prince. That's what Advent prepares us for: that God thought it fitting and right to enter our world through a complex conception story, a messy birth, a willing midwife, and to arrive as a vulnerable baby. God crept in beside us. And as a result there is nothing too complex, messy, or vulnerable about our own lives into which he cannot enter.

So this Advent let's invite in again the Lord of Light, the Prince of Peace, and the King of Love.

---

* Wild Goose Worship Group, *Cloth for the Cradle: Worship Resources and Readings for Advent, Christmas and Epiphany* (Wild Goose Publications: Glasgow, UK, 1998).

2

PREPARING FOR
THE END OF TIME

Thank God We Know Not the Time

*A*longside preparing ourselves to celebrate the birth of Jesus at Christmas, the other major theme presented to us in every Advent is also preparing ourselves for the return of Christ at the end of time. Some of us will recall that during Advent in 1999, when some thought that they were about to usher in a new millennium, a few Christians declared that the end of the world was nigh and that Christ would return on his two-thousandth birthday.

They seem to subscribe to the old adage that "one should never let the facts get in the way of a good story!" Here are the facts.

First, the new millennium began on January 1, 2001. A baby is not one when it is born. But that's a minor point. Second, Christianity took over the Roman calendar in what we now call the fourth century of the Christian era. At Rome in 526, a scholarly monk named Dionysius Exiguus compiled a list of the dates of Jesus' birth, death, and resurrection. He assigned dates in the new Christian calendar for each of these events. Given the tools at his disposal, he did an extraordinary job. However, we know from other historical sources and from the New Testament, where it mentions who the various Jewish and Roman rulers were in Palestine and Rome, that Dionysius was four years out with his dating. The church became aware of this mistake in 1582, but to correct it, the world would have lost four years! So we have all lived with it ever since.

Even if Jesus were going to return on his two-thousandth birthday, we can safely assume that Christ knows the year in which he was born and that even if we got the year wrong, he would have known he was meant to return in 1997!

In every generation, we have had people tell us that the sun, moon, stars, wars, famine, tidal waves, and earthquakes all demonstrate that Jesus is about to return. Clearly, we are still waiting. If only the Christians who give out these dire predictions would take as seriously Jesus' words: "But about that day and hour no one knows, neither the angels of heaven, nor the Son, but only the Father."

The earliest Christians thought that Jesus would return quickly and spectacularly. They were surprised that the first generation of Christian believers was dying without seeing it all happen. Given the terrible suffering they were enduring for Christ, the early Christians no doubt hoped that the end of the world would be soon and would demonstrate to their oppressors that they were not foolish to cling to faith in Jesus Christ. They knew that there was no point professing faith in Jesus Christ unless our daily behavior reflects his kingdom. They knew that their faith would cost them something, maybe everything. Indeed most of us who are godparents do not know that the role of the godparent comes from the first century in the church when Christians left Jewish and pagan families to join the new community in Christ's name. If they were martyred, their children could not go back to their non-Christian families, so "in God's name" another mother and father swore to raise these martyrs' children as their own. And they did. Even though the church no longer uses the term *godparent*, but rather the clinically sounding *sponsor* for this role, the names *godfather* and *godmother* survive. People like it and so they should. Its history is as privileged as is the invitation here and now.

I haven't got a clue when the world will cease to exist and Christ will return in glory. I don't want to know. I do know and believe that the Lord returns to us every time we love, forgive, share, are compassionate, generous, and sacrificial toward one another. It may not be as grand as dancing suns and tidal waves, but the heroic love of a parent for a child, a spouse for their sick partner, and the first world sharing with the third world are spectacular enough for me to believe that Jesus' kingdom comes every day, in every hour, at every moment because Christian's live out their baptismal vows.

Imagine if the approximately 2.18 billion Christians lived out their baptismal commitment to Christ in their daily lives: the world would be transformed and Christ would come in spectacular fashion.

At its best, this season of peace on earth and good will to all people can be a taste for us of the kingdom of God that is both present among us and still to come.

The Unsettling Sound of Silence

In Advent and Lent, we hear much about John the Baptist. He is seriously overexposed. In fact, many preachers run out of creative things to say about him fairly early on. Yet, in the New Testament, he is the figure who points to both the "here and now" and the "yet more to come," so we can see why he is given to us as a central character. His role in the life of Jesus is more complex than some of us were ever taught in grade school.

Some New Testament scholars argue that Jesus did not just go to the desert and pay John the Baptist a visit, but that he was his disciple for a period of time, and later made a break from him. In the Gospels, John the Baptist emerges as a fierce character, opting out of towns and villages and heading to the desert to preach a harsh repentance, fasting, and penance. It was an austere lifestyle.

No matter if Jesus was John's disciple or if he went to the Jordan for a day visit, Jesus did not follow John's lead. He returns to the desert on a needs-only basis. Primarily itinerant, Jesus' mission was to be in villages and towns, proclaiming a repentance of mercy, love, and compassion. I am pleased I follow Jesus.

Throughout Lent and Advent, however, John in the

desert is held up to us as the way to go. Given what I said earlier about how, until the tenth through the twelfth centuries, the Advent season was in fact a later Lent (both five weeks long, both marked by fasting and penance, and both giving the faithful a day off halfway through), we can see why the church returns to the Baptist in the desert in both seasons.

Have you ever been into a desert, a real one? Nearly 70 percent of Australia is semiarid or full-on desert. It's not hard to find a wilderness where I come from. And one of the most religious moments of my life happened there.

In June of 1984, I did a pastoral placement at Quilpie, which is 1,029 kilometers (640 miles) inland from the coast. The then pastor, Fr. Jeff Scully, was one of the finest priests I have ever met. On Sunday morning, June 24, the parish celebrated the Feast of the Body and Blood of Christ, and later that day, Jeff and I climbed into his truck and set off on his "country run." This "run" was a 500 kilometer (310 mile) round trip. It took three days, running rough roads to Eromanga, Adavale, Toompine, and Eulo. These places are as outback as they sound. At the Toompine hotel, after the very devout local faithful celebrated their Sunday Mass on Tuesday, we did a Corpus Christi procession around the pub. It was the most moving one I have ever attended. The drinkers in the bar were not actually imagining things that day!

On Wednesday, as we were heading home, we had a flat tire. It was dusk. Three things hit me in the middle of the desert: with no light pollution, the canopy of the stars was as clear as it was overwhelming; when the new tire was fitted, Jeff and I just sat out there for ages listening to the sound of silence; and I felt incredibly vulnerable. I was pleased to drive home, back into town.

Maybe that's why we are encouraged to go to the desert in Advent: for clarity, to listen, to touch our vulnerability. Going to the desert, and all it represents, is a very powerful experience, but we need to approach it carefully and knowingly.

With good cause, the figurative desert in Christianity has always been associated with ascetic practices in the spiritual life. These are only ever a means to an end; they are never ends in themselves. Once we lose sight of their purpose, we can get lost in the desert of our penance. This is a very dangerous place to be.

In the church these days, some people think our theology and spiritual practices have become too soft, a bit wooly. In some regards they may have a point, but these commando Christians may be following John the Baptist more than Jesus Christ. Truly living a life of mercy, love, and compassion should hold enough tough love with which to be getting on.

Penitential acts do not change God. God is unchanging. They change us so that we might in turn change our world for the better, so that it reflects the kingdom that Christ proclaimed.

Even though we have the ancient and venerable Christian tradition and witness of the desert fathers and mothers, St. Anthony was very careful about the centrality of moderation, joy, and compassion that should mark the Christian life in an actual or figurative desert. The story is told about a monk who went to Abba Poemen and asked him, "When we see brothers who are falling asleep during the services, should we arouse them so that they will be watchful?" Poemen said, "For my part, when I see a brother falling asleep, I place his head on my knees and let him rest."

In and through our preparations in Advent, we have to keep focused on what it is we are actually seeking: to enable the Lord of Life to be reborn in us this Christmas, and that our public lives will mirror the growing freedom of our private prayer. Sometimes, for the love and joy of Christmas to flow and flower in us, we need to confront the blocks that get in the way of us living the life of grace.

It is good to head to our figurative desert this Advent for clarity, to listen, and to touch our vulnerability, but our time there should be marked by encountering God's mercy and compassion and an assurance of his personal love for us. It should also see us reinvigorated to be sent back with Christ to our figurative city to live and proclaim Christ's kingdom wherever and however we are.

At the Hour of Our Death

John the Baptist is not the only saint in the Christian tradition who straddles the here and now as well as pointing us to the end of time; Mary, the Mother of God, does as well.

Our Lady is the symbol of Advent, patiently saying yes and literally laboring with God to bring salvation to birth at Christmas. And while she never figures in any of the end-of-time scenarios in the Gospels, in our devotional life, she looms large in being there at the end of our own time on earth. In the Rosary, we ask her to "pray for us now, and at the hour of our death." As first among the saints, she also points to God, who will never be outdone in fidelity, hope, and love.

My most affectionate and early memories of devotion to the Rosary started when I was eight. Many of my summer holidays were spent at my Uncle Maurice and Aunty Claire's ranch in the outback of Australia. I come from a large extended Irish/Australian Catholic family. They took Genesis 1:22 seriously when God said "be fruitful and multiply." On that side of the family tree, I have thirty-two first cousins.

Maurice Leonard was the patriarch of the nine Leonard children. He used to call up each family before the school holidays and invite all his nieces and nephews for the vacation. There could be up to ten cousins on holiday there at any one time. It's only now that I think of Aunty Claire cooking, cleaning, and washing for that crowd.

Uncle Maurice and Aunty Claire were married in 1948. Every day, from that day until Uncle Maurice died a few years ago, they said the Rosary. And even though the nightly devotion was falling off in our homes as children in the 1970s, when we went to their ranch for holidays, we would all kneel after dinner and recite the five decades. Because Maurice and Claire had become so used to each other's patterns of prayer, they had a very distinctive way of "giving out" the Hail Mary and responding with the Holy Mary. Uncle Maurice would say, "Hail Mare mingum, blest la jim." By the time Maurice got to *mingum*, which I assume was "among women," Claire would start, "Whole a may mem." And so it went: "Hail

Mare mingum, blest la jim/Whole a may mem." They were speaking in tongues long before it was trendy!

If any of the cousins were too slow, and actually said, "Hail Mary, full of grace…" Uncle Maurice would say, "Speed it up Rich." So, if it you can't beat 'em, join 'em, and so we all said "Hail Mare mingum, blest la jim. Whole a may mem." Of course, Claire and Maurice rightly understood that the Rosary was a mantra prayer. We are not meant to meditate on every word of every prayer, but to use the words to still our minds and focus on the chapter of Jesus' life in each mystery.

The other features of Uncle Maurice's Rosary were what he called the "toppings and tailings." These were all the prayers before and after the Rosary. Do you remember them? They felt like they were longer than the Rosary. We said the Apostles' Creed, the Benedictus, and the Magnificat before, and then prayers to the Sacred Heart, for the conversion of Russia (that worked!) and for the protection of the pope (that worked too!).

About eighteen years on from when I started vacationing on the family ranch, I decided to enter the Jesuits. One of my other cousins, Paul Leonard, who went to that ranch as often as I did, took me out for dinner. Given what I was doing with my life, matters religious were on the agenda. Out of nowhere, my cousin said across the table, "Hail Mare mingum, blest la jim," to which I immediately replied, "Whole a may mem." And back and forth it went for a while until the waiter asked us which Eastern bloc country we came from!

During the meal, we recalled lots of memories of those summer holidays, including saying the Rosary. At one stage my cousin said, "There was one weird prayer Uncle Maurice used to say in the tailings. Do you remember it, when he hit his chest?" "What was weird about it?" I asked. "Well it's a bit strange, don't you think, to hit your chest and call out, 'Say G'day to Jesus,' and then reply, 'Have mercy on us.'" Now, this is a little Australian moment, but my uncle had a very broad Australian accent. What my cousin thought was "Say G'day to Jesus" was in fact "Sacred Heart of Jesus." And at that moment, I could hear my uncle saying it and could well understand how a young boy thought his uncle was "Saying G'day to Jesus," to which we all called back, "Have mercy on us." This was a tough religion!

This Advent, it might be good for us to reclaim a very healthy devotion to Mary as first among the saints, a companion to us in the journey of faith, a prophet, and as our mother. Let me tell you where it happened for me, and why saying "at the hour of our death" means so much to me now. First, however, I need to tell you that when I was in grade four of my Catholic School, Sr. Mary Wenceslaus, RSM, was our music teacher. She came into class one day and taught us the twelfth-century Latin prayer to Our Lady, *Salve Regina*. Hold that thought.

On August 15, 1975, eight members of a village in the mountain country well above the capital of Chile were arrested by the military police. They were accused of being terrorists and organizing labor unions. They were innocent of the former and proudly guilty of the latter. For months the villagers tried to find out where the men had gone and why they had been taken away. As we now know, abduction, torture, and illegal imprisonment were daily realities for Chilean people under General Pinochet.

Word arrived in November that the corpses of the parish councilors could be found in Santiago's morgue. My friend, Sr. Catherine, was an Australian nun working in that parish. She took the mothers of the eight men to the morgue in Santiago. Catherine later wrote to me, "Richard, you could not imagine what we found in the morgue. There were over a hundred corpses piled high on each other and our mothers had to roll someone else's son over in an attempt to find her own. And as the mothers searched, they began to weep loudly, realizing how evil we can be toward one another. As they wept, they prayed the Rosary. As one mother, and then another, found her son, they called out more desperately, 'Holy Mary, Mother of God pray for us sinners now, and at the hour of our death.'"

Catherine's letter continued, "For years I rejected devotion to Mary because I felt oppressed by the way generations of men in the Church presented her—blue veils, white skin, always smiling, a perpetual virgin and yet also a mother, an ideal I could never achieve, but one to which I was told I should aspire. In the experience of the village mothers, however, the distortions of who Mary was for a poor and suffering world faded away. Far from feeling distant from their devotion, I found myself praying with them, knowing that Mary was with us in our shock, anger, and grief."

The letter went on, "What happened next was indescribable. Twenty soldiers stood by and watched nine women load eight corpses into my truck. They never lifted a finger to help us. We could only get seven out of the eight in the back, so one of the mothers cradled her son in her arms in the front with me. The journey took four hours. On the long trip home, they prayed the Rosary again and again. As the mother next to me said at one stage, 'We can only pray with Mary at times like this because she knows what it's like to bring a child into the world and claim his dead body in her arms.' There was Mary—right beside me."

Twelve years later, in 1989, Catherine died of hepatitis in that village. Her family had been trying to get her to come home for months, but she lied about how ill she was and said that she had everything she needed there. The only consolation for Catherine's family was when a letter arrived from the mothers in the village. When I had it translated from Spanish into English, it read, "We want you to know that we were with Catherine when she died. We would never have let her die alone, for she was one of our children too. We often prayed the rosary with her. She seemed to like that, thumbing the beads she used ever since she brought us back with our boys. We have buried her next to our sons and put on her tombstone the line she asked us to inscribe: 'Mary my friend, my companion, and mother of the poor, pray for me.'"

In 2010, I was the first member of either Catherine's family or friends to go to Chile. I caught a bus from Santiago, and nearly five hours later, alighted at 2 p.m. The five surviving mothers were waiting for me. They took me immediately to the cemetery, and there I found Catherine's grave among eight men who were killed in 1975. There was the inscription on her grave in English and Spanish. We all stood and wept. Then one of the women asked me to pray. They had very little English. All I could say in Spanish was, "*Lo siento, no hablo español.*" But then, like a good steward who brings out of the storehouse both things new and old, I remembered Sr. Mary Wenceslaus.

Salve, Regina, Mater misericordiae,
vita, dulcedo, et spes nostra, salve.
Ad te clamamus exsules filii Hevae.
Ad te suspiramus, gementes et flentes
in hac lacrimarum valle.

Eia, ergo, advocata nostra,illos tuos
misericordes oculos ad nos converte;
Et Iesum, benedictum fructum ventris tui,
nobis post hoc exsilium ostende.
O clemens, O pia, O dulcis Virgo Maria.*

By the end of that ancient love song, we were all singing and crying and hugging.

This Advent, may Mary pray with us that we will be made worthy of celebrating again the first coming of her Son, and be ready for his second coming into our lives, here and now, and at the hour of our death.

Entwined for Eternity

I am not sure whether the Advent wreath has made a debut or a comeback. It was never a feature in the Ad-

---

* The work was composed during the Middle Ages by a German monk, Hermann of Reichenau, and originally appeared in Latin, the prevalent language of Western Christianity until modern times.

vent liturgies of my childhood. I was an altar boy and I would remember seeing it or lighting the candles. I was always looking for something to do, for it made Mass go more quickly. In fact, the Advent wreath has a very complex history.

Wreaths go back to the Etruscans, the ancient Greeks and Romans, and symbolized all sorts of things, from one's office or status in society, a success or an achievement (the forerunner of the ribbon, medal, or plaque), to a fashion statement.

By medieval times, wreaths had come to be used in three ways: as symbols of the harvest; as the completion of the circle of life at funerals; and as an anticipation of Christ's coming during Advent. As best as we can make out, in Europe, during dark December, green branches were found and woven together as a promise that spring was on the way, and candles were lit as a metaphor for Christ's birth, piercing through the darkness of our sin. It may well have had an echo of the ancient relationship between Advent and Lent, in that the wreath can also symbolize Jesus' as-yet-unthorned crown.

This largely German ritual was confined to people's homes. In this regard, the ritual lighting of the candles is also a nice quotation of the ancient Jewish custom of the kindling of the Sabbath candle or, better still, the lighting of the menorah candles during the Feast of Dedication, Hanukkah, which, and not by accident, often coincides with our Advent.

The Puritans did not like the pagan origins of the Advent wreath, so they opposed it, but it persisted, and as German Catholics and Lutherans migrated all over the world, they took this domestic ritual with them as well. It caught on, and though it is not an official part of the Catholic Advent liturgy, it has come to be a legitimate custom. It is a rare cathedral or church that does not now light the Advent wreath.

It's striking that while harvest rituals and their accompanying wreaths have largely gone, the funeral and Advent wreaths remain as strong as ever. During Advent, the wreath entwines both ideas: the completion of our life-long journey; along with the final unveiling, or the apocalypse, of Christ.

Without doubt, the most nagging question confronting Christians, as they contemplate the end of their lives and the end of the world, is, what will the next world be like? Let me speculate on what may lie beyond the veil.

Some time ago, Pope Benedict XVI surprised a few people when he suggested that heaven, hell, and purgatory may not be places where we do time, but could be experiences through which we arrive or pass. I think he is right, not only because time and space are elements of this imperfect world, and not the next world, but also because this opens up interesting ideas about what these experiences might be like, and how rich the Catholic tradition is in this regard.

When I think of what the hereafter might be like, I turn by way of analogy to the magnificent parable of God's mercy in Luke 15:11–24, the prodigal son. Here is a Jewish boy who commits two of the worst sins he could commit: he squanders his patriarch's inheritance, and is so down on his luck that he would have gladly eaten what the pigs are eating. Then he decides to go home and make up with his dad. I think that is what death is like for all of us, the final journey. This image is poignantly evoked in the final Holy Communion given to our dying, which is called *viaticum*, which literally means "food for the journey."

Meanwhile, in the story, the father watches and waits on the road all day, every day, for any sign of the son's return. It is worth noting that the father did not go and club the son over the head and haul him home. The son had to put himself on the road home, which is similar to what happens when we die. We begin the final journey home. And when this extraordinary father sees him, he rushes out, kisses him, and calls for a party, even before the kid has had a chance to finish his well-rehearsed apology. That has to be heaven. For some of us who do our best, though we also fail, we get the basics right and God, who knows our heart and has accompanied us as we have labored under the difficulties with which we have lived, does not even want the apology. We are welcomed home.

For some of us, however, the meeting with God may be personally painful because, as I have argued throughout this book, God takes our free choices very seriously. So when the extraordinary Father sees some of us, he rushes out to meet us, but when we are face to face with love itself, we are aware of the many free and knowing times we have been destructive toward ourselves, others, and our world. At that point, we will be allowed to start and finish the well-rehearsed apology, asking, indeed, in some cases begging, for forgiveness. It will cost us dearly to own what we have done, because it will be so stark, and it will cost God to forgive us. But because the Father is full of mercy and compassion, we will be cleansed, or purged in love. Echoes of this approach are found in Pope Benedict's words when he met, in 2008, with the priests and deacons of Rome during Lent: "Today we are used to thinking: What is sin? God is great, he understands us, so sin does not count, in the end God will be good toward all....It's a nice hope. But there is justice, and there is real blame. Those who have destroyed man [*sic*] and the earth cannot sit immediately at the table of God, together with their victims."

Finally, I think there may be some of us for whom the Father will rush to meet us, but when we are face to face with love itself, we will do what we have freely and knowingly chosen to do all our lives—we will reject God's love and walk away, the ultimate sin, which no doubt reflects how our lives on earth were spent. That has to be hell—the abyss—to see the face of God (of love itself) and walk away from it because we always have. And the Father painfully respects our choice, even this one to reject him. As the pope says, "It is precisely the last judgment of God that guarantees justice....We must speak specifically of sin as the possibility of destroying oneself, and thus also other parts of the earth." But like the pope, I do not think this final group is large. "Perhaps there are not so many who have destroyed themselves so completely, who are irreparable forever, who no longer have any element upon which the love of God can rest, who no longer have the slightest capacity to love within themselves. This would be hell."

As painful as death and grief are, and the end of time may be, the Advent wreath symbolizes both the completion of the cycle of life and our hope in Christ's reign beyond time and space, where we hope and pray that our parting from those we have loved in this world is not a definitive "goodbye," but more a "see you later."

Swept Off Our Feet

Jesus and Satan have an argument as to who is the better computer programmer. Eventually, they agree to hold a contest, with God as the judge. They set themselves before their computers and begin. They type furiously for several hours, lines of code streaming up the screen. Right before the end of the competition, a bolt of lightning strikes, taking out the electricity. Moments later, the power is restored and God announces that the contest is over. He asks Satan to show what he has come up with. Satan is visibly upset, and cries, "I have nothing! I lost it all when the power went out." "Very well, then," says God, "let us see if Jesus fared any better." Jesus enters a command, and the screen comes to life in vivid display; the voices of an angelic choir pour forth from the speakers. Satan is astonished. He stutters, "But how? I lost everything, how can Jesus' program be intact?" God chuckles and says, "Ah... because Jesus saves!"

When in Advent we are asked to focus on Jesus coming at the end of time, it is all about being saved, an event that has happened, is happening, and will be consummated at the end of time. I am not being personally provocative in using that marital imagery in this regard. It is invoked everywhere in the writings of the fathers of the church: the final consummation of Christ's return. It is drawn from Revelation chapters 12, 19, and 21, where Christ, the bridegroom, takes the church, his bride, as his own, and consummates the marriage between heaven and earth.

For some modern ears, this imagery is just too earthy. I think celibates may have sanitized religious imagery way too much. Jesus and the writers of the New Testament had no such hesitations: brides, grooms, betrothals, marriages, wedding banquets, and consummations are alluded to throughout the twenty-seven books of the Christian Scriptures.

For others the image is too patriarchal, but it is good to recall that we are never coerced into the life of grace. God does not force his love upon us; we are seduced, enticed, and invited. We are free to accept or reject Christ's offer, so this marriage metaphor is embedded in a mutuality of self-giving love.

Now, I know nothing about the consummation of a marriage, though I do like the fact that, for a Church which can be seen to be "obsessed" with sex, as Pope Francis put it, we have one sacrament that is not valid until and unless you consummate your marriage with your wife or husband after the ceremony. No sex, no sacrament!

From my vast and idealized ignorance, I have always liked this imagery because it is embodied, tender, and generative. These ideas challenge some sterner and harsher ones in regard to the end of time that often prevail in our imaginations. The just judge is also a tender groom on the wedding night.

The reason I like the metaphor of the groom over the judge is because so many of us think we will have to plea bargain with the judge to get the best possible deal out of this life, and the life yet to come.

It reminds me of the story of Daniel, who went to his mother demanding a new bicycle for Christmas. "Danny, we can't afford it," she said, "so write a letter to Jesus and pray for one instead." "Dear Jesus, I've been a good boy this year and would appreciate a new bicycle. Your friend, Daniel." Now, Danny guessed that Jesus really knew he was a brat, so he tore it up and tried again. "Dear Jesus, I've been an OK boy this year and I want a new bicycle. Yours truly, Daniel." Danny knew this wasn't true, so he tore it up and tried again. "Dear Jesus, I've thought about being a good boy so may I have a new bicycle? Daniel."

Finally, Danny thought better of making these false claims and so ran to the church. He went inside and stole a small statue of Mary and ran out the door. He went home, hid it under his bed, and wrote this letter: "Jesus, let's face it: I've broken most of the Commandments, tore up my sister's doll, and lots more. I'm desperate. I've got your mother, Mary; if you ever want to see her again, give me a bike for Christmas. You know who."

There is a little bit of Danny in all of us.

The image of us "doing a deal" with God is so prevalent in our theology and prayer that we can find ourselves lapsing into it all the time. "If you make me well, God, I will lead a better life." "I will return to Sunday Mass if I pass my exams." "I will raise my children Catholic if I have a fine day for my wedding." This is all dreadful stuff. And some of our Catholic forebears have to take some responsibility for giving us these images so forcefully.

The problem with this bargaining theology is that it cannot be reconciled with the Advent story. We don't save ourselves. We cannot earn salvation by doing good works or prayers or penance. And, as difficult as it is to hear, we cannot save anyone else. That includes our children, spouse, grandchildren, parents, or friends.

Jesus saves us. Jesus saves us from death. Jesus saves us from living lives devoid of purpose and meaning, and Jesus saves us from the worst things in ourselves.

Our prayers, good works, and faith are the responses we make to the salvation of Christ we claim here and now, and as we prepare for the life to come. And how we live is the way by which those we love will find the gift of God's salvation for themselves.

God has not held back one thing in his love for us. By becoming one with us in our flesh, Christ, the bridegroom, assures us of his saving love. He has shown us everything that can be shown about how we can live lives of sacrifice, justice, and love together, and how to transform our world for the better.

The Scriptures tell us from the beginning of time, to the preaching of John the Baptist, to the life, death, resurrection of Jesus Christ, and to the ongoing work of the Holy Spirit among us today, that we have a God who risked everything so that we might know love and life in this world and in the next. We hold and proclaim, in season and out of season, a God who emptied himself of power and might and came to us as a baby.

That's not the profile of a deal doer. So let's leave behind any vestige of God as a benevolent dictator. Advent is the story of God as a lover who is seductive, self-giving, tender, generative, and consummating. Christ, our groom, waits patiently for our acceptance of his proposal for a saving love that will last for eternity.

I Will Never Forget You

As a trainee Jesuit priest, I had to teach for two years in a Jesuit high school. On the whole, I really enjoyed the experience and learned a tremendous amount from it. That is, except for Year Ten religious education class. Year Ten was made up of boys aged fifteen to sixteen, and I had them for religious education in the last period every Friday for a year. Who thought that was a good idea?

Many fifteen-year-olds have a studied disinterest in almost everything, but when it came to religion, my Friday class of twenty-four adolescent boys did not even try to feign interest: too late, too much, not relevant. That class was my glimpse of purgatory.

One day, trying to be proactive and provocative, just to disprove the theory that the class was in fact brain-dead, I walked in and said, "What would you think if, when we die, we find out there is no God, and that religion is simply a social and human construction?" There was no immediate reaction, so I asked again, probably a little too pleadingly.

Just as I thought my brain-dead theory might be right after all, a hand in the back row shot up. It was Joshua, the biggest cynic in the room. He said with the self-assurance that only an adolescent can muster, "Well, sir, apart from the fact that if there is no God, and after death we won't be thinking about anything at all, if your idea is right, then you are going to look a lot more stupid than we are."

Josh was just warming up. This kid, who had shown not an iota of interest in my class at any stage that year, said, "Mind you, I have always wondered what will survive us when we die, and what it means to say that we will meet God face to face, when we won't have a face at all." Joshua just won the Year Ten theology prize. He was already a good philosopher, and now he was becoming a theologian. The class then came to life.

In a matter of moments, my twenty-four boys became young men. Far from being disinterested in death and matters eternal, they were fascinated by it. Rather than run from mortality, they were anxious to give me their theories about what, if anything, survives us after death, and how Christian faith helps or hinders them in expressing their hopes and desires.

One of the things I noticed was that most of the young men used the term *soul* to speak about that which is eternal. I am sorry to say that, until that moment, it was not a big part of my own theological vocabulary, so they didn't get it from me. I would have used *spirit* to indicate the same thing. But they didn't. They were comfortable with the idea of a soul.

Later when I was reflecting on what had happened in that class, it struck me that in recent years, while the spiritual conception of a soul and its use in our religious language has waned, the word *soul* persists in ordinary conversation. That's why the young men may have been comfortable using it. Many nonreligious people use this most religious of terms to describe another person. We often hear how others are lonely, distressed, or lost souls. It can be said that someone has a "beautiful soul" or that a piece of music, a painting, or other work of art was "soul stirring." We describe mellow jazz as "soulful" and still alert others to distress by an SOS, "save our souls." These uses of the word reinforce St Thomas Aquinas's teaching that the soul makes us human, and sets us apart from other animals. Nearly all the great religions of the world believe in a soul, or its equivalent—something that survives the annihilation of the body in death.

In Advent, when we are asked to not only prepare to receive Christ at Christmas, but also at the end of time, Josh's question is still among the most important ones to ponder. What survives us? How can we know and be known by Christ? What is a soul?

I have come to the opinion that whatever else might characterize the soul, memory is an integral part of it. Our memories survive us.

I have done several funerals of people who have suffered from Alzheimer's disease. These are rarely very sad occasions because the family invariably says that they "lost" their loved one months or years before. Why? Because they felt increasingly that their loved one could not remember anyone or anything. We believe in caring for the body from the womb to the tomb, because we believe that human dignity must always be respected. There are now theories about how even memories of the circumstances of our conception and birth may have a bearing on the way we live our lives. It is also apparent that even when people seem to have lost their memory, or are unconscious, that there is some recognition of some things at a very deep level. I am struck, for example, how people who suffer from Alzheimer's disease, and cannot remember who they are or where they are, can still construct perfect sentences in their native language, and sometimes in other languages they have learnt in their lifetime. Language is a profound exercise in memory, even when the meaning of the stated sentences can be quite confused.

Memory as a constitutive element within my soul means that when I meet God face to face, I will remember who I am and how I lived, and God will remember me. This fits into that long and venerable Old Testament tradition about God remembering us, and God instructing the Israelites to remember his fidelity and goodness to them. To this day it is a great sin for a Jewish man or woman "to forget." It also complements the biblical idea of death as the final act of purification; thereafter, we have no more pain and are at peace.

In the New Testament, we find what German theologian Johannes Baptist Metz called the "dangerous memory of Jesus," where his life, death, and resurrection show us both the cost of being his disciple and that God will never forget us. At the Last Supper, Jesus instructs us to do this meal "in memory of me." As we have seen earlier, this is an *anamnesis*. It not just about celebrating this sacred meal again, but of enacting and embodying what it signifies and achieves in us.

Finally, St. Augustine, in book 10 of his *Confessions*, reflects on the nature of our soul and says that it has three constitutive elements: memory, understanding, and will. It is, however, "to the fields and vast palaces of memory" that he finds "a vast and infinite profundity…(and) infinite multiplicity." Augustine knows that memory is the key to knowing God because he wonders how we can search for God if we do not already have an archaic memory of God in our soul.

So, I find myself in good company in these speculations that what will be with God for eternity is our soul in its purified memories. Even on a pastoral and personal level, it is a comfort for us to think that we may be reunited with those we have loved who have died before us, because we will remember each other.

I am hoping to meet my one-time student Josh again. He died of leukemia in 2011, aged thirty-six. I presided at his Requiem Mass. When I saw him the week before he died, we recalled the Friday theology class we shared twenty years before. We spoke again about the nature of the soul, and we shared our best thoughts on the topic, but now there was a greater human urgency and deep emotion in the conversation. "I hope you're right about the soul, Father," he said, "because I am about to test your theory earlier than you."

I want to remember Josh and want him to remember me because, whatever else will happen at the end of time, we believe God will never forget us.

3

THE CHRISTMAS SEASON

God Is Good with Mess

After I was ordained and worked in a parish for a while, I was sent to Melbourne to begin my ministry in communications. One of the part-time jobs I took on was to be the chaplain to an inner-city Catholic grade school. The school is a great mix of children from the wealthier inner-city terrace houses and from the high-rise housing projects.

Sacred Heart School had an eighty-two-year-old religious sister who was in charge of pastoral care. She was the wonderful grandmother most of these kids didn't have. Sister used to organize the passion play during Holy Week and the nativity play during the festive season. In the weeks leading up to Christmas, it was third grade's turn (eight years of age) to perform the nativity play. I was asked to be the guest of honor.

When I arrived, Sister told me that she had trouble with the boy who was playing the innkeeper because he had his heart set on playing St. Joseph. "Ahmed is an Islamic boy, a refugee from the projects, and I really thought I should at least have a Christian, if not a Catholic boy, playing St. Joseph." Rehearsals had not gone well, but she was sure that everything would be fine in the performance. What could go so wrong? Whatever happens, anyone who does not enjoy eight-year-olds playing out the story of Jesus' birth needs some therapy.

The whole school was there along with all the parents of Year Three. In the front row of the school hall was the principal, Sister, and me.

Everything about the play went along as expected until the moment when Mary and Joseph arrived at the inn. Joseph knocked on the makeshift wall that was the inn's door. The innkeeper, whom we could clearly see, yelled out gruffly, "Who's there?" "I am Joseph and this is my wife, Mary, and we have nowhere to stay tonight and she is having a baby." (Having a baby? If her baby bump was anything to go by, that girl was having octuplets!) The innkeeper did not budge. Sister lent forward in a loud stage whisper and said, "Ahmed, you know what to do, darling. You know your lines. Open the door and make your very important speech." He didn't budge.

So Sister told Joseph to knock again. The innkeeper barked more angrily, "Who's there?" We got Joseph's speech again, but the little innkeeper didn't move. The tension was rising in that room now, so Sister lent forward again and in a stronger voice said, "Ahmed, your Mum and Dad are here, darling, and they will be so proud of you. Now just play your part and make us all proud."

Sister then told Joseph to knock for the third time, and he gave out his speech again. Before Ahmed could decide what to do next, a loud bass African voice came from the back of the room, "Ahmed, you open that goddamn door or I'll belt your bum!" I turned around to see the largest human being I have ever seen.

Ahmed's father, Mohammed, was a refugee to Australia from Sierra Leone. He was six feet eight inches tall and told me he weighed in at 238 pounds (seventeen stone) of solid body mass. So proud was he that his son had a starring role in the Christmas play that he was dressed in his magnificent white celebratory kaftan with a small white cap on his head. Now, however, he was coming down the aisle toward the stage, and every adult there was thinking, "Open the door, open the door, open the goddamn door, because I think your bum is going to be belted by this guy and is going to hurt."

Someone intercepted Mohammed as Ahmed opened the door and said plaintively to Mary, "You can come in," but then shouted at Joseph, "But Joseph, you can piss off!" With that, Joseph burst into tears, and the shepherds and the three wise men started a fight with the innkeeper "because he said a rude word." Sister stood up, turned to everyone and said, "This wasn't the way it was supposed to go." It took ten minutes to restore peace.

It was the best nativity play I have ever seen. God is good with mess. The first Christmas must have been a very messy affair. I know there is a long tradition that holds Jesus' birth was as miraculous as his conception, but it pushes the bounds of the doctrinal claims to Jesus' full and true humanity to say his birth was not like yours and mine.

I find it even more moving to reflect on the experience of a thirteen-year-old girl and her nineteen-year-old husband travelling about a hundred miles (160kms) from Nazareth to Bethlehem in the final weeks of her pregnancy. There is nothing in the Gospels that suggest that Mary and Joseph were not at the normal betrothal ages for first century Palestine: twelve to fourteen years for girls, seventeen to nineteen years for men.

On arrival, they find themselves homeless, and at least in one tradition, Jesus was born in a cave or stable where the animals were housed. Imagine the smell. This is far from the sanitized image we have on our Christmas cards or of which we sing in our carols. This is Emmanuel—God meeting us in our mess and leading us out of it.

No one predicted the way God would send us a savior. No one knew the day or the hour of his coming. No one foresaw that he would be born a homeless person. No one envisaged that the first witnesses to his birth would be illiterate, non-temple-going shepherds from nearby fields. And while some waited for a mercenary to overthrow the Romans, and others held their breath for the procession of a great and grand royal king, heaven and earth became one in a poor, defenseless baby.

The nativity tells us that God is okay with our mess, not to simply leave us there, but to show us the Way, Truth, and Life that lead us to the fullness of life in this world and in the next.

Finding My Family

Do you know what Gospel the Church has selected for the Christmas Vigil Mass? It is the genealogy of Jesus. As theologically and liturgically appropriate as this idea might look on paper, only someone who has never had to contend with thousands of largely unchurched children at Mass on Christmas Eve could even begin to think that this Gospel might work during that liturgy. Wisely, most pastors I know bring forward the shepherd and angels from the Gospel for Midnight Mass.

There are two versions of the genealogy of Jesus in the New Testament: Matthew 1:1–17 and Luke 3:23–38, and both are incredibly revealing texts, and stunning for Christmas reflection.

You might have seen some of those genealogy shows on television, where they trace someone's family history and roots. Matthew and Luke are the earliest versions of it I know, but we may not like to find some of the people listed there in our family tree!

Writing for a predominantly Jewish-Christian audience, Matthew goes back to Abraham, the father of faith. Luke, writing for a predominantly Gentile-Christian audience, goes back before the chosen people to Adam. As they progress, the names are almost identical between Abraham and David and then they vary considerably, coming together in Joseph, who is not announced in either list as the father of Jesus but as the spouse of Mary, the mother of Jesus.

I want to focus on Matthew's genealogy. The power of what it reveals about Jesus' birth is lost on us today, but it would not have been lost on its first audience. There are forty-two names in the list. He leaves out several significant Old Testament people that should be there, such as Ahaziah, Joash, Jotham, and Jehoakim. It would appear that Matthew wanted forty-two generations from David to Jesus, because of the symmetry of multiples of seven, the perfect number.

Even in the numbers, there are echoes of creation, of God doing great things. There are in fact six days of creation, not seven. On the seventh day, God does nothing but have a day off and rejoice in what he has made. It is the oldest labor law in the world, and it is the reason why even the most lowly worker has official entitlements to a day's rest each week. The number forty-two, six times seven: in the procession to the Messiah, we have the perfect creation, but it is via some less-than-perfect means.

In Matthew's list we find heroic models of faith and self-sacrifice: Abraham, Isaac, Judah, Nashon, Jehoshaphat, Uzziah, Jotham, Hezekiah, Josiah, Zerubbabel, Joseph, and Mary.

There are several names of people who are named in the Old Testament, but that is about it. We assume they were honorable men: Perez, Hezron, Ram, Amminada, Salmon, Boaz, Obed, Jesse, Joram, Shealtiel, and Abiud. And then things get really interesting.

Jeconiah was king during Israel's worst chapter, when they were deported to Babylon as slaves. There is Jacob, who started out badly but came good. David and his son, Solomon, start out well enough, but end up as very mixed blessings for Israel. Urriah, Abijah, and Asa were punished for displeasing the Lord. Rehoboam, Ahaz, Manasseh, and

Amon were ruthless, murderous tyrants. I am not sure anyone would find these men in the family tree.

We have eight men we have never heard of, or at least they are not recorded in any of the books of the Old Testament: Eliakim, Azor, Zadok (not the famous one), Achim, Eliud, Eleazar, Matthan, and Jacob (not the famous one). Maybe they were in the oral history of the time, but they are lost to us now.

But wait! It gets better still: the women. Only five women are mentioned or alluded to by Matthew. All of them conceived their child in what could only be described as complex circumstances: Tamar, the wronged widow of Genesis, gets her own back by seducing her father-in-law, and was vindicated for her courage. Rahab was a Canaanite woman in prostitution who bravely aided the Hebrews to enter the promised land by spying for them. Ruth starts out life as a Moabite. They were despised by the Jews. She converts to Judaism but is a poor, childless widow until she meets Obed and ends up being the great-grandmother of King David. Bathsheba is not mentioned by name, but commits adultery with King David, becomes pregnant, and then David has her husband killed to cover up his sin. Marrying David, her abuser, she becomes the mother of Solomon. Finally, there is Mary, who conceives through an immaculate conception. So these five women all become mothers in extremely unusual circumstances.

The genealogy of Jesus is helpful because, at the very start of the Gospel, it places two things at the center of the Christmas drama: family and complex human beings.

On a theological level, because of the first Christmas, we have been welcomed into God's family in this most intimate of ways. We do not have an austere and remote god. We have a God who has taken our flesh in the incarnation and, through the saving love it affects, we have been welcomed into the very life of God's own self: Father, Son, and Spirit.

In the fifth century, St. Augustine said that because of the first Christmas, the Trinity was revealed to us as mutual fidelity, sacrifice, and a tender love. Maybe the very best Christmas gifts we can give in the coming days would be to decide to forgive someone in our family who has hurt us (even if they are dead), or to tell those who actually love us that we love them, or to do a genuine act of kindness for a family member, or to be generous enough to the poor that they might know that we recognize that, in Christ, we are all one family.

The weeks after Christmas are the times when I do more pastoral counseling than any other time of the year, with those who have been humiliated at Christmas lunch by members of their family. Their stories are sometimes harrowing, and even if half true, they are a tragic way to have spent December 25. These events have nothing to do with Christ's birth. Maybe the most sacrificial and loving thing a few of us can do this Christmas is not to go home to people who do not respect us as they should. Maybe our "family" at Christmas this year might be made up of those friends who are bound to us by mutual faith more than ties of blood.

That said, the genealogy of Jesus is also about complex human beings. Here is where God chose to come among us, right into the complex story of every family tree. Therein we find the great and the good, the cruel and criminal, those lost to history, and women who are found pregnant through the most complex of circumstances. In God, all these themes combine to become the symphony of our salvation. And that can be true in our own families too.

If we are sometimes applauded and cheered for the good we do, we belong to the family of God. If we are booed and hissed for the things we get wrong, then we belong to the family of God. If, in time, we will be forgotten by almost everyone for what we have achieved while on this earth, then we belong to the family of God who will never forget. And if we have been, or are, in a messy situation, then we belong to the family of God. Because of the first Christmas, there is no pain God cannot heal or set to rights.

No matter if this Christmas we are sadly alone, or with family; if this is a happy time of year, or a stressful one; if there are fights at lunch or we have a great reunion of relatives and friends; as a result of the first Christmas, God comes to where we are and as we are. And how can I be so sure?

The genealogy of Christ tells us that we belong, it's okay to be needy, that we will be remembered, and that God will heal. Because of that first Christmas, there is nowhere, no home, and no heart that Christ will not enter. All we have to do is welcome him in, so that good can eventually triumph over the most evil of actions, that good can come from unrecognized fidelity, and that even in events that first appear to be a disaster, the revelation of love can emerge.

Walk on the Wild Side

I was ordained a priest in North Sydney in December, 1993, where I was serving as the deacon and then assistant priest at the Catholic Parish of Kings Cross. It was, as you could imagine, a very colorful parish. Soon after my ordination, I went to Queensland to say Masses there and at the Catholic communities to which I had belonged over the years.

I returned to Kings Cross on Christmas Eve and was told by my seventy-year-old Irish parish priest that I would be presiding at Midnight Mass. What he did not tell me is that while I was away, Esme, our eighty-year-old sacristan, had gone all over Sydney to buy every meter of gold lamé available to make me a set of vestments for the occasion.

I saw it for the first time when I arrived in the sacristy. I had to wear it, of course, and when I put it on and looked in the mirror, with Esme beaming beside me, I looked like a Christmas tree.

Midnight Mass was packed to the rafters, and by the way this Catholic congregation sang, it was fairly clear that most people were full of more than one type of Christmas cheer!

Soon after Mass began, five tall men in white blouson shirts walked all the way down the aisle to the only available seat in the church—the very front pew. It was clear that only one of them knew what to do at Mass, and he instructed the others to do as we do.

After Mass, at drinks on the pavement outside the church, I went over to these men and welcomed them to the parish. "Hello, I'm Fr. Richard Leonard. I haven't seen you here before and I'd just like to wish you a very happy Christmas." To which one of the five turned to me and said, "Father, if you don't mind me saying so, you wear your frock divinely." At that moment I turned into the butchest priest in Australia. "I don't get any kicks out of wearing this stuff, you know. I normally get straight back to the sacristy and get it off there." And as soon I said that—I really wished I hadn't.

It transpired that my five new parishioners were from the now defunct *Les Girls Show*. They were at 2 Roslyn Street. St. Canice's is down the road at 28 Roslyn Street. That night they had done the usual show at 10:30 p.m., but, as a Christmas special, they still had a late, late show to do at 3:00 a.m. Mark, the only Catholic among them, had convinced his colleagues to "get some religion and come to Midnight Mass."

They had enjoyed Mass so much that Mark suggested that I get a few of the other Jesuits and come up the hill at 3:00 a.m. "Seeing we came to your show, Father, you should come to ours." I declined the offer, but Mark explained that, in case I changed my mind, there would be tickets waiting for me at the door.

As they were about to walk up the hill, the one who told me I'd worn my frock divinely said to me, "Father, if ever you want some help to 'tizz up' any of your little church outfits, just let me know, because I am a wonderful designer, and I know I could do a number on you." At that moment, I had visions of coming out from the sacristy the following week in plums, feathers, and a tiara.

When I got back to the presbytery, I told three young visiting Jesuit students the entire story. It transpired that none of us has been to *Les Girls*. Guess what happened next?

We were late for their show, too, but the tickets were waiting for us at the door, there was a table at the back, which suited me just fine, and we were served complimentary drinks. To my relief, no one had seen us go in, and I decided we would be leaving early as well. St. Ignatius has lots to say about things done in the dark—but we won't go there for the moment.

The girls put on a great show and everything was going along quite nicely until the end, when Mark, now in his Marcia persona, went to the microphone to wish everyone a Happy Christmas. He told the audience that to celebrate Christmas, the girls had been to Midnight Mass in between the late shows and that, as a result of that, "we'd like to welcome our local Catholic clergy." With that, a spotlight came on our table! I stood and waved to all my new parishioners.

Marcia then told the crowd that I had sung at Midnight Mass and invited me to "come up here on stage to lead the crowd in a rousing chorus of 'O come all ye faithful.'" As I walked to the stage, all I could think of was how I was going to explain this to the cardinal archbishop of Sydney, my Irish Jesuit parish priest, my provincial superior, and, worst of all, my mother when she found out!

Do you have any idea who goes to the late, late show of *Les Girls* on Christmas morning? That is, other than young Jesuits! But there I was, not three weeks ordained, at 4:30 a.m. on the stage of *Les Girls* at Kings Cross, leading a very dubious group of our compatriots in singing, "O come let us adore him, Christ the Lord."

Within six months of that night, I had buried three of the five men who came to Midnight Mass. One committed suicide in March. We had to break into his flat in Darlinghurst to find him and the gun. The second man died of a heroin overdose in St. Cancie's public toilets. I found him dead in the cubicle when I was locking up. The last man died of HIV/AIDS in the Sisters of Charity hospice in June.

After his mates died, the fourth man wanted to get out of Kings Cross and start a new life. The local Jesuits helped him reestablish himself in rural New South Wales. I baptized him in 1996 at St. Canice's, did his wedding in 2000 at St. Canice's, received his wife into the Catholic Church last year, and earlier this year, at the only church they knew and liked, I baptized their triplets.

Mark, the only Catholic on that first night at the church, now works full-time with homeless teenagers in Sydney. He was once homeless himself, being ordered out of his family home at sixteen, when he told his parents that he was gay. He and his partner remain devout parishioners of another inner-city Sydney Catholic parish, and work with at-risk homeless young people who live on the streets.

There would be some Catholics and Christians who would think those men had no place coming to Midnight Mass. They would almost certainly believe that I had no place going up the hill that night, of all nights, if any night. On both scores they would be horribly wrong. The reason the good news touched these men's lives for the better was not just that they came to us, as good as that was, but also that I took a risk and went to them. Risk taking is the story of Christmas.

In all the accounts of Christmas we have in the New Testament, we hear the angel begin her announcement of Jesus' birth with the words, "Do not be afraid; for see—I am bringing you good news of great joy...to you is born this day…a Savior, who is the Messiah, the Lord" (Luke 2:10–11).

Fear is a terrible thing. It cripples us into passivity. It ruins our memories of past or present events, and it undermines dignified, trusting, and respectful relationships. Broadly speaking, we fear four things: God, nature, other people, or something in ourselves. For some people, it can be a combination of these things, or, tragically, it can be all of them.

To any degree that fear rules our lives, let's hear God's greeting this Christmas: "Do not be afraid," and take some risks in our faith, hope, and love. St. Paul tells us that love drives out all fear. Thus we remember the birthday of a man whose life, death, and resurrection showed us the way out of our fears.

On any day when we face down our fears and live our Christian life to the full, we'll discover that Christmas is a moveable feast. And how can I be so sure? Because, on Christmas morning, when I was only three weeks ordained, I found that the liberating presence of Christ had preceded me at 4:30 a.m. to the stage of *Les Girls*. As a result, I was to see the power of God's amazing grace.

So let's face down our fear, take a few risks, and find a voice to

> Go tell it on the mountain,
> over the hills and everywhere
> Go tell it on the mountain,
> that Jesus Christ is born.

4

THE HOLY FAMILY

A Tough Act to Follow

*C*hristian art has not served us very well in terms of giving us an image of the Holy Family. From medieval times, Joseph is portrayed as being at least eighty, Mary is very young with perfect white skin and, usually, Jesus has brown golden curls, blue eyes, and a knowing smile. This scene has more to do with Europe than first-century Palestine, but it has gone all over the world. Don't tell anyone that the Holy Family were far more black than white, and that Joseph was certainly not ninety-two years of age.

In the medieval period, it was incorrectly assumed that older men lost their sexual desires, so an ancient-of-days Joseph got Christianity around the issue of his sexual desires. Joseph was old enough to be a great provider for Mary and Jesus, but too old for anything else. Case solved. Well, not quite.

For fourteen years, I was the regular celebrant of the nationally televised Mass in Australia. It goes to homes and hostels for the aged. It airs at 6 a.m. on Sundays. One Sunday, I proclaimed that difficult Gospel where Jesus condemns adultery with the heart. I was young and stupid, but that doesn't explain why, at the start of my homily, I looked down the barrel of the camera and said, "If you're feeling capable of adultery, then at this stage, I think even the Lord would understand!" Though I don't entirely regret it, what possessed me to say such a dumb thing? In the week that followed, I received scores of letters from women in nursing homes, Catholic and otherwise, who not only took me to task for what I had said, but for my ignorance of their context. One woman rightly admonished me, "You have no idea how predatory some older men in aged care facilities are, do you?" I didn't. But now I do, and I am grateful to know it. So making St. Joseph an elderly man does not mean he is free of the demands and choices involved with celibacy.

We know only the barest facts about the Holy Family. Joseph was eighteen when his fiancée, Mary, thirteen, potentially caused great scandal in the neighborhood when she conceived a child by the power of God before the wedding. They were a poor family from Galilee that was harshly administered by the occupying Roman Army. The night Jesus was born, they were homeless. Matthew tells us that the Holy Family knew what it was like to be a refugee. They were very devout Jews. At one stage, we know that it took them a day to realize they had lost their child, and then another two days to find him. On this last point, we would now be running Mary and Joseph into Child Services!

By these traditions, the Holy Family has much to say to those in our world who are teenage mothers and fathers, are poor hard-working religious people, are refugees, or are so-called people of color. They give consolation to any parent who has ever lost a child in a market place, or been through the heart break of losing a child in death. In fact, the more we put halos on the Holy Family, sadly, the less we seem to be able to connect their family experience with our own.

Most families are about being generous, loving, stable, and faithful. They stand for security, roots, and identity. Our world needs stable strong families more than ever before. Families, however, also fight, can be envious, they break up, and, tragically, the family home is the most common place for child sexual abuse. For all our Western wealth and technology, I think it's often very hard to have a happy and balanced family life today. So what's the secret?

A recent survey of couples who have been together between fifty to seventy years, and who regard their families as "happy," gave as the top three attributes: love, gratitude, and forgiveness.

No surprises that love tops the list, but as one respondent said, "Our family is happy not just because of *any old love*, but because we live out sacrificial love, where you don't get your own way all the time—and that's okay. It is a love that is happy to give and take." Another said, "As a husband and wife, we have had to lead by example in living a love that genuinely wants to put the other person or a child first." No wonder it works: sacrificial love is the core of the gospel.

The second attribute is gratitude. I thought this survey response was priceless: "I can't think of a time in my sixty-year marriage and family life that my husband hasn't said 'please' and 'thank you.' I have never felt taken for granted. From making a cup of tea to having a baby [I must admit that I smiled at the difference in effort between these two activities], he always sincerely says 'please' and 'thank you.' It was a good habit we all got into in our family, and I notice my children insist on it from their children too, and they say it to their husbands and wives. It's a simple thing, but it says 'I value what you do and who you are.'" *Please* and *thank you* could be the fastest disappearing words from the English language, and yet they give respect and dignity. If you have got out of the good habit (there is such a thing as a good habit) of saying please and thank you to those around you, then here is your simple and profound New Year's resolution.

The third attribute is forgiveness. In this regard, I always think of the outrageous motto of the 1970 hit film, *Love Story*: "Love means never having to say you're sorry." That might have been fine for Ryan and Ali, but it is not the gospel of Jesus Christ, and it's a key to unhappiness. For Christians, and for happy families, love means we can and want to say we're sorry and that the other person in the family can, and wants, to forgive.

One respondent said, "In our fifty-year marriage and forty-nine years of family life, we could never pretend that forgiveness has been easy. It has never been a magic wand we've waved over deep hurts and harsh words. Forgiveness does not deny reality, it deals with it." Another stated, "From small annoying things to a few big moments, genuine forgiveness has been essential for us facing a crisis and not getting trapped there. It has enabled us to learn, deal with it, grow, and move on."

In our complex family lives, no one can pretend that forgiveness is easy or that it is a magic wand we wave over deep hurts and harsh words, but revenge and spite, so endemic in society, are the antithesis of what Jesus taught and lived out. True forgiveness does not deny reality, it deals with it. St. Ignatius Loyola was a wise man who knew about the drama of human living. He said that sometimes we are not ready to forgive someone else, so the best we can do is pray for the desire to *want* to forgive them. He says we go as many steps as we need to, but that being a forgiving person is one of the hallmarks of following Jesus. Sometimes we have to start by forgiving ourselves and those who have died. I know there are a few people in my life who have hurt me deeply, and I pray for the desire to get the desire to want to forgive them. At least I am heading in the right direction.

The Holy Family is a tough act to follow. There has only been one family whose membership included a canonized saint, someone immaculately conceived, and the Son of God. But there is some evidence in the Gospels that they, too, had to walk the talk in the same way our often complex families do. This feast is not about emulating an almost impossible example, but to be very practical in asking if our own families and communities are sacrificially loving, grateful, and if we genuinely want to forgive each other when the going gets tough.

No one promised us that family life would ever be easy, just that the rewards would be worth all the efforts involved. May Jesus, Mary, and Joseph pray for us.

Love Is in Deeds not Words, but Words Matter

The Feast of the Holy Family is about faithful love that looks after the most important people in our lives.

I have often been with people on their deathbed when they speak about things they have left undone and would have liked to have achieved in their life. No one ever says that they wish they had spent more time at work. No one says they wish they had made more money. But many people say that they wish they had told those they love that they loved them. We shouldn't assume that our families know about our love for them if we haven't said it. Here is my story.

In my last year at Catholic high school, a wonderful priest, Fr. Ray O'Leary, gave us our annual retreat. At one stage, we were given an extract from a book upon which to ponder and pray entitled, *Why Am I Afraid to Love?* At one point, it said, "Don't leave this world not having told the people that you love that you love them."

I came home from that retreat on a mission!

I don't come from a particularly demonstrative Irish Catholic Australian family. I was almost seventeen, but I had never told my mother, brother, or sister that I loved them. They had never said it to me. My father had died when I was two years of age. So now I had a personal challenge.

My sister was then working with Mother Teresa in Calcutta, and my brother was working interstate. I sat down and wrote them letters. "Dear Peter/Tracey, I just want to tell you that I love you." I have never heard back from either of them!

That left my mother. I stayed in one Saturday night and after dinner, while she was watching the national news at 7:00 p.m., I was in my bedroom. With my heart pumping and my tummy churning, you would swear I was about to ask her to marry me. But I approached the sunroom, and then blurted out, "Mum, I have something important to tell you." My mother, not taking her eyes from the screen, casually said, "Oh yes, what's that?" "Mum," I responded, "I've never told you this before, and it's very important that I tell you tonight."

My mother slowly turned off the TV and turned toward me. Now I could tell that there were two hearts pumping and two tummies churning in that room. Later my mother was to tell me that, at that moment, she thought I was about to say one of two things: "Mum, I have got a girl pregnant," or "Mum, I'm gay." Whichever one it was, she was saying to herself, "Keep calm, keep calm, keep calm."

I plucked up all my courage and came straight out with it. "Mum, I just want to tell you that I love you."

"Is that it?" she said.

"Yes, before I die, I wanted to tell you that I love you." I said.

"Oh my goodness, you aren't terminally ill are you?" she earnestly asked.

"No, but I just want to be man enough to tell you that I love you, and do."

Such was my mother's relief, she looked up and said, "Goodness me, I hope so," and then promptly turned back on the television.

I remember walking back down to my room thinking that I didn't think it was supposed to go like that. There were no violins playing, no warm embraces, no statements like, "At least one of you three ingrates has turned up to tell me that you love me." No, none of that happened. What did occur was that my brother and my sister wrote to my mother saying, "We received these very strange letters from Richard." My mother wrote back, "Bully for you! I've had it in person, but don't worry because it must be another phase he is going through." Hopefully, it is a phase I will never get over, because the ease of saying it is at the core of being a disciple of Jesus.

One of the problems with love is that we have devalued the currency of the word. We say we love our car, our house, and ice cream. We even say we love our dog or our cat. But we cannot love things because they cannot love us back, and as much as we can have deep affection for pets as our companions, this relationship is not as robust, conscious, free, and mutual as loving another human being.

Some of us regularly tell people that we love them when we actually don't love them, for we love them out of habit or obligation. It may be for sex, but we don't actually mean it, and we know it. When we use the word insincerely, it doesn't help us when we then hear others tell us that we're loved, or even when God whispers it in our ear continuously. We may not trust it.

Let's agree only to tell the people that we actually love that we love them. And how do we work out who those people are? Ask one question: For whom would you die? In my experience, that shortens the "I love you list" considerably, and if your dog and cat is on that list, you need therapy immediately.

It is this form of love, which would give something, maybe everything for those we love, which is at the heart of the Feast of the Holy Family. Their love for each other and for the world ended up demanding everything.

Christian love is also practical. It is not just about warm feelings, as important and good as they are, but our love has to lead to concrete choices: Love is in deeds not words (1 John 3:18). So much so, I have a small problem with some people who seemingly tell just about everyone that "I love you." In fact, I know some fifteen-year-olds whom I hear tell their parents that they love them, and then speak to their fathers appallingly, or treat their mothers with contempt. At that point, I want to say, "You might love your parents one day, but you don't right now. You can say it as much as you like, but if your actions do not follow the profession of love you make, then you are wasting your breath."

Love is not just about feeling good; it is about doing good. Funerals are where I can get the most steamed up about this. Up gets a wonderful young adult, who, through a veil of tears, eulogizes his grandfather, who has been a magnificent man: "Oh Pa, we loved you so much, so much. I don't know what we are going to do without you. How are we are going to keep going without you?" To which I want to say, "Are you for real? I have been seeing Pa in the local nursing home for the last three years and he used to weep to me that, despite the fact that they lived in the same city, his children and grandchildren rarely came to see him. The staff of the home confirmed that this was true. And now he has four hundred people at his funeral and an otherwise terrific young person professing love and wondering how he will get on without him. I sometimes want to ask them all, 'Where have you all been for the last three years?' We are all busy. It certainly takes time and trouble, and sometimes there is nothing in it for us except being with a gift and a giver. But why take the day off work to farewell the dead when you could have seen the person while he or she was living?" I know which I would prefer. Where we put our bodies is the point of our true love. As Jesus said, "Where your treasure is, your heart will also be." That sorts out what and whom we actually love very quickly.

In this regard, I especially like 1 Corinthians 12, which is the most famous wedding reading in the world. I have had brides and grooms who discounted having it read at their ceremonies because "everyone has that." I always suggest that the couple pray over the reading by taking out the word *love* and putting in their own names: *Jack and Jill are patient and kind. They are not envious, boastful, proud, arrogant, or rude. They do not insist upon his or her own way and are not irritable or resentful. They do not rejoice in wrongdoing, but rejoice in the truth. Jack and Jill's love will bear all things, believe all things, hope in all things, and endure to the end.* This tends to counter the "everyone has it" factor and brings home to all just how practical Christian love is supposed to be.

The best way to honor today's feast is to do something about the faithful love it celebrates. If we show it, we should be able to say it. So write a letter, make a call, or go and see them, but let's pluck up our courage and tell our families that we love them. It's too late once we're dead.

And the best news is that when we profess our love to our families, we'll see that the Holy Family is a moveable feast.

MARY, MOTHER OF GOD

Saying Yes

*H*ave you ever been to Ephesus, in modern-day Turkey? Many people go there for the world heritage Roman ruins. Others go because it is a study in climate change. Ephesus used to be a famous sea port, but it is now fifty miles (eighty-one kilometers) inland. It was from this important city that Paul seems to have written his First Letter to the Corinthians, and to here that he wrote his Letter to the Ephesians. Some scholars believe that the community of the beloved disciple was here, from which came the Gospel of John.

A very few of us might also go to Ephesus to see the ruins of the building wherein one of the most important councils of the early church was held.

When the Council of Ephesus gathered in June 431, it was by no means clear which way the bishops would vote in declaring Mary to be the Mother of God. In fact, this council was not called to talk about Mary at all. This council was called to refute Nestorianism, which held that the human and divine natures of Jesus were separate. The council defined that Jesus was at the same time truly human and truly divine, and went on to declare Mary to be the *Theotokos*, the God-carrier, which has come to be called, Mother of God.

The Council of Chalcedon in 451 settled the question of Jesus' humanity and divinity by saying that he was "perfect in divinity and perfect in humanity," and "like us in all things but sin."

Curiously, it is at Ephesus where a wonderful piece of Christian enculturation also took place. We know from other ancient Roman texts that the great local cult was to the goddess Diana, under her preeminent title *Stella Maris* (Star of the Sea). The ruins of her temple are there to this day. As the city converted to Christianity, the earliest Christian leaders transferred that title to Mary, and it is with us to this day, especially in schools, colleges, and churches on or near the coast.

In the deliberations at the Council of Ephesus, two touchstones were established for orthodox belief: What do the people believe and how do they pray? Today it is spoken of as the *sensus fidelium*, the sense of the faithful. This was a watershed moment. The vast majority of the bishops affirmed that their people believed that Jesus was truly God, but they also attested to the fact that their congregations believed that Jesus was truly human. Why? Because, while Jesus had done miraculous things, taught with authority, and been raised from the dead, they knew he also shared in the most important element of being a human being: he was born of a woman, Mary of Nazareth, who, therefore, was not just a mother of a man, but also the mother of God.

I like the literal translation of the Greek proclamation about Mary. She is the "God-carrier." Mary carried the God-man, Jesus. In AD 270, St. Gregory Thaumaturgus said of Mary, "You are the vessel and tabernacle containing all mysteries....All that was hidden from preceding generations was made known to you; even more, most of these wonders depended on you." Although we might use different language now, I like the idea of the tabernacle, not only because it links us so directly to our Jewish heritage, but because given our grand churches and sometimes expensive, physically remote, and fixed tabernacles today, the first carrier, the original vessel, was a Palestinian teenage girl who moved, was frail, and human. She was carrier of God.

And it all starts with the second greatest yes in history, after Jesus. In his film *Jesus of Nazareth*, Franco Zeffirelli pictures the annunciation this way: Mary is asleep at night when a gust of wind opens a high window. Afraid of all the commotion, Mary gets up and starts to pray. As she prays, we see her face change and her body bend over. With tears in her eyes, Mary looks up through the window to the moonlit sky and simply says, "Be it done unto me as you have said." The swirling wind dies down at once.

Mary is not coerced to say yes. Although blest by God, she was a free human and could have said no. That's what makes her yes even greater. Mary's fiat sets in motion the entire Christian drama.

In fact, it is a disputed theological point whether Mary could have said no. The Jesuits and Dominicans have been fighting about it since 1588. If you think you have ongoing fights with your neighbors, come join religious life! It is called the debate over free will and grace. The Jesuit position is the following: While Mary could have said no to the angel, what makes her yes richer and stronger is that she was given human freedom. The Dominican position is this: Such was the grace of the immaculate conception that Mary had to say yes to the angel. In 1582, Pope Clement VIII said that both views are right, now shut up. (Of course, the Jesuits are right, there is no question about that!)

God was not bound by Mary saying yes or no. He had other options. So she is invited by God, not forced, to be the mother of Jesus Christ.

Because of the Mother of God's yes, then our yes to her Son is possible. Each and every time we are invited to deepen our relationship with God, we are invited, not forced. While God can be seen to be an irresistible force or as the most seductive of seducers, nothing obliterates our free will.

This freedom is enshrined in all our ceremonies of Christian commitment: marriage, holy orders, and religious profession where, before anything else happens, our freedom to choose is sought and confirmed. This is not a liturgical nicety. We do not become God's marionettes, but, through the grace of being called and our responding in love, we are invited into an unequal but mutual and respectful relationship. Like God did with Mary, we are treated like adults.

What does Luke's Gospel say was Mary's first response after saying yes to carrying God? It is the Magnificat, and there is nothing sentimental and pious about this extraordinary hymn. In it, Mary proclaims that God, through Jesus, will show strength through scattering people's pride, tearing down the mighty from their thrones, and raising up the poor in their place. God will fill the hungry and send away empty the rich, who have not shared. In this the promise of salvation will be fulfilled for *all* people. This is not Mary-lite or Mary dripping in piety. It is a strong woman saying yes that will change the world forever.

For us, too, especially in the Christmas season, this feast is an opportunity to reflect on what God has done for us in Jesus Christ, and to enter more deeply into the mystery of who God is calling us to be right now. In what ways do I let Christ be born in me? In what ways do I need Christ to be born in me?

May Mary, the Mother of God, bear us to her Son as she carried him to us, so that we may keep saying our saving yes to the saving love of Christ.

There Is Nothing Told about This Woman but...

The best contemporary Marian hymn I know is by the Australian Jesuit, Christopher Willcock. Chris translated into English a poem of the same name by the French Jesuit, Didier Rimaud: *There is nothing told about this woman.* It says,

There is nothing told about this woman, but that....

It's a very big "but," for the poem goes on to recount most of the events about Mary in the New Testament.

> She had once become engaged...
> She brought into the world...
> She searched for three long days...
> She at Cana was a guest...
> She was standing by the cross...
> She was one in prayer with those...

The antiphon after each verse sings,

> On this day all earth and all paradise
> join in naming you happy and blessed.
> Virgin Mary, blessed are you.*

In 1974, Pope Paul VI told us in *Marialis Cultus: For the Right Ordering and Development of Devotion to the Blessed Virgin*, that if we wanted to have a sane and lively devotion, then we should start with the Gospels. The Christmas season and the Feast of Mary, the Mother of God, provide no better context than to do just that.

There are ten scenes in the New Testament wherein Mary is portrayed: the annunciation; the visitation; the nativity; the presentation of the child Jesus in the temple; the flight to Egypt; the losing of Jesus in the temple; when Mary goes to bring Jesus home from his public ministry; the wedding feast at Cana; the crucifixion; and Pentecost.

In a few places, I have already spoken about the an-

---

nunciation, but no wonder the reaction of a thirteen-year-old girl, having been invited into the drama of the definitive intervention of God into the world, was to be *diatarasso*; this word in Greek, while sometimes translated as "perplexed" or "troubled," is even stronger still and might better be rendered as "greatly agitated." Luke tells us that Mary is initially and understandably panicked. Who wouldn't be? After being reassured, however, she says yes, which is all the more incredible because she had no detailed idea of where that yes would lead her. It was a pure act of faith and trust.

The tradition has not been kind to St. Elizabeth. She is always presented as being ninety-nine years of age. Given that in Jesus' day most people were dead by the age of fifty (that's why three score and ten is such a colossal age), Elizabeth, who could have been old at thirty-six, may have been going through menopause, during which she becomes pregnant, which is not an unknown reality to this day. But the visitation is one of the most moving scenes in the Gospel. On a human level, here are two cousins, unexpectedly pregnant in the most extraordinary circumstances, meeting and offering each other greetings and support. We can see the scene and feel the bond. They meet in the mountains, where God has always been manifest to the Israelites. Elizabeth embodies the Old Covenant made to Israel, and she carries John who will be the herald of the Messiah. Mary embodies the new, and final, covenant in Jesus. Elizabeth recognizes what is happening here, and she embraces all that God is doing for the world. She has tasted the promise of God and now sees its fulfillment.

Earlier, we spoke at length about the traditions around the nativity of Jesus. The problem is that most of the customs around Christmas are not to be found in the Gospels. It is a case of "not letting the truth get in the way of a good story." The customs related to Christmas have more to do with much later customs. In Matthew and Luke, there is no donkey, no arrival on Christmas Eve, and no innkeeper. All that is said is that Jesus was laid in a manger because there was no guest room, *kataluma* in Greek. It could have been with relatives or friends. The one thing we do know is Jesus was born in poverty, for a manger is a stall for feeding cattle. Mary and Joseph had no access to a fancy birthing suite. Furthermore, no angels sing at Jesus' birth. Later, we are told they "praised" God, so they might have sung out a few numbers as they did! There are no kings who come from any specific country, simply "Magi," or wise men. There could have been two or several of them, but we get three because they bring three gifts. And they don't present these gifts at the manger, but they visit sometime later, after Jesus had been presented at the temple in Jerusalem. By that time, the text calls Jesus a child, not a baby. There is no mention of mid-winter or snow. In fact, the census more likely took place in the spring. The first we hear of December 25 as the date for Jesus' birth is in the mid-fourth century, which, by one account, is approximately the time we Christianized the pagan sun festival, Saturnalia; by other accounts, St. Augustine among them, the date is nine months to the day after his conception and death, March 25.

The presentation of the child Jesus in the temple tells us that the Holy Family was devoutly Jewish. They did everything prescribed by the law, which stipulated that forty days after a child's birth, the parents should present their baby in the temple as an act of thanksgiving. Here we meet Simeon and Anna, who foretell that just as the Israelites waited for forty years to enter the promised land, so now the time of waiting, of formation, is over. Israel receives the promised Messiah.

Only Matthew relates the flight into Egypt, and so many think it more a theological story than a factual one. On every level, this is one of the most terrifying stories in the Gospel. At least I hope so. Not because Jesus is saved from a tyrant. So far so good! But what about all the other babies who were slaughtered? Didn't God care about them, too? What were they, collateral damage? Alternatively, Matthew is beginning to draw his picture of Jesus as the new Moses. Just as Moses was saved as a child and goes to Egypt, so is Jesus in even more dramatic terms. By the end of the Gospel, just as Moses gave the law, Jesus is the law. At the center of this dramatic story is Herod, who is locked in fear. Matthew will later portray Pilate in a similar way. The result of being threatened by who Jesus is, or how he lives his life, results in death—Herod's slaughter of the innocents in the first case, and later, Pilate's murder of Jesus. Matthew tells us that the enemy of the Christian life is fear, so this is the moment to take flight from fear and embrace freedom.

The story of losing the child Jesus in the temple has so many delicious details. Jesus is twelve (reminiscent of the twelve tribes of Israel) when the holy family goes up to Jerusalem and loses the boy on the way home. It took them days to realize they had lost him. These days, Mary and Joseph would be reported to Child Social Services. But they find him on the third day (the work of the Lord) teaching the scribes—another new Moses moment in Mathew's Gospel. And they did not understand why he had done this to them.

In Mark 3, we have the curious episode of Mary and the family of Jesus going to take charge of him because they thought he was out of his mind. He was making a stir. This is not a Gospel that fits easily into the Christian "family values" rhetoric today. Jesus does not go out to see his family but says that his mothers and brothers are those who do the will of God. This passage is comforting to any parent who has difficulty understanding what their son or daughter is sometimes on about.

John only mentions the mother of Jesus twice: at the first of his signs, the wedding feast at Cana; and at the last and definitive of his signs, the lifting up on the cross. On the surface, the feast at Cana tells us that Mary and Jesus liked a party! John 2:6 says that each of the six water jars held twenty to thirty gallons, for a total of 120 to 180 gallons of water (680 liters). Given today's wine bottle, that's seventy-five dozen or nine hundred bottles of wine. Wine in the Old Testament is always a symbol of joy. When the steward tastes, it is not just good wine, as *kalo* in Greek is sometimes translated, but it is excellent or the best wine. On a deeper theological level, Cana tells us that the mother of Jesus knows that when he is present, we are never left to feel ashamed, that the eternal banquet has begun, and where Christ is, joy flows beyond all imagining.

Sadly, we are so used to the scenes of the crucifixion of Jesus, we have domesticated its horror. Imagine what it is like to watch your child capitally punished. That's what Mary does. And just to bring it home some more, imagine Jesus did not die on the cross. Imagine he died in the electric chair, was shot by a firing squad, or given a lethal injection, and there was his mother watching, unable to do a thing about it. Praying here with Mary is about all those things in life that are criminally and horribly unfair, and our power-lessness to stop them. Mary has something to say to any parent who has ever lost a child in death, before or after birth.

At Pentecost, fifty days after Easter Day, here is Mary in the center of the earliest church as it starts its mission to witness and preach the hallmarks of the final and greatest of the biblical jubilees: we have been set free in Christ to reap a new harvest, and to declare that humanity is debt free.

On this the greatest feast in honor of Mary, these ten episodes enable us to let go of a plaster statue image of Mary and embrace, as a flesh and blood woman, our mother, sister, prophet, and friend. Though uniquely gifted by God for her mission, she was fully and truly human. Mary is not God. She needed God's redemption in Christ. This poor, simple Jewish woman is the preeminent disciple of the kingdom Jesus proclaimed. She has something to say to anyone in our world who is a teenage mother, a poor hard-working religious person, a refugee, and a so-called person of color. Like Jesus, Mary was not white. She gives consolation to parents who can't figure out their children, have ever lost a child in a market place, or been through the heartbreak of losing a child in death.

On this day, all earth and all paradise join in naming you happy and blessed. Virgin Mary, blessed are you.

6

EPIPHANY

Wonder or Fear

*I*n heaven, one year it was decided that on the Feast of the Epiphany they would have a liturgy that recreated the visit of the three stargazers from the east. The job of the stargazers was given to the founders of three great religious orders in the Church.

Everyone gathered to see St. Francis of Assisi come forward at the appropriate time and lay clay doves before the crib of Jesus. As one, the heavenly host all went, "Ahhh."

St. Benedict was next. He processed beautifully to the crib holding a magnificent bejeweled Bible. On the front of it were the words, "This is your life." Everyone in heaven called out, "Ohhh."

Finally, St. Ignatius Loyola limped forward, not carrying a gift. He walked straight past the crib and then past Mary. Everyone in heaven was aghast and thought, this is so typical of Jesuits: he doesn't know where he's going at liturgy and turns up empty-handed! They watched as he went over and put his arm around Jesus' foster father: "So tell me, St. Joseph, have you decided where you're sending the kid to school? Hang with me and I'll get you a special rate."

When we go to the cinema, we have to suspend our critical sensibilities to enter into the full power of the story. A similar concession is necessary to reap the full benefit of the story of the first Epiphany. Have you ever wondered, for example, why the wise men, who have been guided from the east to Jerusalem, stop there and ask directions from Herod? Surely the star could have kept doing its job and taken them all the way! And why didn't Herod follow the wise men, or at least send a spy behind them? Furthermore, whatever happened to these wise guys? They are the first in Matthew's Gospel to recognize who Jesus is, and yet they vanish from Jesus' life as quickly as they came into it.

Like many screenwriters, Matthew plays with history for another purpose. Like cinemagoers, we're happy to suspend our questions and look beyond the story's details so we can enjoy the profound picture that is being painted for us. And profound it is. These dreaming stargazers in Matthew's Gospel point to the radical nature of the kingdom revealed in Jesus Christ. This story takes on an even more radical tone when we remember that Matthew is writing for a predominantly Jewish community. The people of Israel considered themselves as the chosen people, and they hoped and longed to see the Messiah. Yet here are three Gentiles, to whom the promise of the Messiah had not been made, who are among the first to see and believe in Jesus.

Throughout his Gospel, Matthew is at pains to show how the Jews missed out on recognizing Jesus because they were locked in their fears. King Herod is the first public official to be portrayed in such a way, but he is by no means the last or the least. Pilate suffers a similar fate at the end of this Gospel. Matthew links these two rulers. The result of being threatened by who Jesus is, or how he lives his life, is death—Herod's slaughter of the innocents in the first case, and later Pilate's murder of Jesus.

Matthew's story is also a wonderful interplay between wonder and fear. We are told only five things about the wise men from the east: they follow the rising star, they ask directions in a foreign land, they are overwhelmed with joy at finding the child at Bethlehem, they are warned in their dreams about Herod, and they go home by another road.

Herod, on the other hand, is frightened at the prospect of a pretender to his throne, he whips up fear in Jerusalem with similar anxiety, uses the wise men to find the child, his deceit is uncovered, and he is left without knowledge and more spiraling fear.

In twelve verses, Matthew paints a portrait of wonder and fear. If we are wise followers of the Babe of Bethlehem, we need to be shrewd in dealing with power; keep our eyes on the journey, which mostly brings joy and fulfillment to our lives; believe in dreams;, and pray that we are never so sure of how God works in our world that we miss seeing the very thing we long to behold.

Matthew also tells us that the enemy of the Christian

life is fear. So often our reactions to Jesus can be like Herod's. We can be threatened and frightened. We want to eliminate the voices that call us to live out the reign of God, and remind us of the costs involved. Fear entraps us and infects those around us, and we are often most fearful when we risk losing power, so we lie, become deceitful, and cheat to maintain our position at all costs. As with Herod and Pilate, it all ends in death.

So this story is far more than a travel log of some exotic Persian kings. It is the story of the choices that lie before Christians everywhere. The choice is ours again. In our following of Christ, do we want to live out of wonder or fear?

Glorious Dreams

Last year, some Christian scientists got to work on trying to explain the star that led the wise men to Bethlehem. They came up with a complicated, and no doubt plausible, astronomical theory about how a certain brilliant star may have appeared around the time of the birth of Jesus. Though I was intrigued by their methods, I wondered why they bothered. Matthew's wandering star is not about astronomy. It's religious shorthand for describing how the heavens preside over and guide the events of the world.

The image of a star is used in similar ways in the Books of Deuteronomy, Numbers, the prophet Isaiah, and the Psalms. The Feast of the Epiphany is all about symbols, not science. Reported as a liturgical feast by Hippolytus as early as the third century, it is celebrated twelve days after Christmas, the number itself echoing God's fulfillment of Israel, and then God's going beyond it.

The wise men's star is on a par with the other images Mathew uses. There is an extraordinary event at the center of each of the first three chapters of his Gospel: in chapter 1, Joseph hears the message of an angel in a dream; in chapter 2, the wise men find Jesus by following a star; and in chapter 3, the heavens open and God speaks at Jesus' baptism. By any standards, that's quite an opening to a biography! It's all about the manifestation, or epiphany, of God's glory in the world.

Let's look carefully at where and for whom this glory is revealed. The first instance is to Joseph, while he's asleep in bed. The second is to Gentile astrologers who, by reporting their news to Herod, set up an immediate threat to Jesus. The third instance is to all those Jews who were coming to hear John the Baptist. Within three chapters of Matthew's Gospel, the circles of God's glory revealed in Jesus become more public and change the lives of Joseph, the stargazers, John the Baptist, and those who heard Jesus preach. They will never be the same again.

The Feast of the Epiphany is not an ancient version of Halley's Comet. It is about how God's glory challenges and changes our human hearts. T. S. Eliot got this point in his poem, *The Journey of the Magi*:

> Were we lead all that way for
> Birth or Death? There was a Birth, certainly,
> We had evidence and no doubt. I had seen birth
>   and death,
> But had thought they were different; this Birth was

Hard and bitter agony for us, like Death, our
    death.
We returned to our place, these Kingdoms,
But no longer at ease here, in the old dispensation,
With an alien people clutching their gods.
I should be glad of another death.*

It is this link between Jesus' birth and death that we
celebrate in the Epiphany. In the midst of the extraordinary scene of visiting stargazers, their gifts tell us that the
richness and power of this child's reign will be revealed
through his death and resurrection. When we name the
real threats in our life, we can know the overwhelming joy
of finding the "Morning Star who came back from the
dead and shed his peaceful light on all humanity."

And just when we weren't necessarily expecting it, I
think the Feast of the Epiphany is very practical. The first
thing we learn is to trust our dreams, and learn to remember and analyze them.

In the Scriptures, dreams are highly valued forms of
communication between God and humanity. Joseph, the
eleventh son of Jacob, is the famous dreamer of the Old
Testament, as well as being the interpreter of other people's
dreams, notably the Egyptian pharaoh. But he is not on his
own. King Nebuchadnezzar, the prophet Daniel, and King
Solomon are just three more famous figures whose dreams
have a dramatic impact on the destiny of Israel.

There are plenty of people who dream dreams and
see visions in the New Testament too, culminating in the

* From *Collected Poems 1909–1962* (Faber, 1974), by permission of the pub-
lisher, Faber & Faber Ltd.

Book of Revelation. In Matthew's Gospel, Joseph dreams twice; the Magi are told in a dream not to reveal the whereabouts of Jesus to Herod, and Pilate's wife warns her husband to have nothing to do with Jesus.

There are a few curious features to God's revelation in all these dreams. God is not religiously discriminating in whom he visits. Joseph is a devout and righteous man, but the Magi are Gentiles and Pilate's wife is a Roman pagan. The same holds true for Pharaoh and Nebuchadnezzar in the Old Testament. God visits whomever he needs to to get the job done.

In and through these dreams, people can have religious experiences that lead to right action. In the Scriptures, these dreams were taken seriously enough for them to be the basis of some important decisions. In almost every case, biblical dreams save lives or tell of how to guard and protect.

The Epiphany tells us that if God has created us with an unconscious and subconscious life of which dreams are a sign, then God has a purpose for this gift, and they can be used for good. Long before Carl Jung, dreams were a gateway to an inner mystical world. It would be a mistake to dismiss them as a fad of the new age. If we never take them seriously, if we decide that God cannot or does not talk to us through our subconscious world, then we will never know their importance. The scriptures tell us that ignoring dreams, particularly persistent ones, has destructive consequences.

However, like the Scriptures themselves, dreams need careful interpretation and discernment. Where are our dreams leading us? What protection and warning could they be providing for us? A key is found in the dreams of the wise men. After they see Christ, they are warned to not return to Herod and to go home "another way." It's a delicious detail. One path, which they could not see, would have been to death, but they trusted their dream to follow another path to life.

The Epiphany is the story of the choices and dreams that lie before all Christians everywhere. To follow Jesus' rule is to keep our eyes on that star that lights the path to have the courage to live out his gospel, to carry our crosses, whatever they be, and to trust that God will remain faithful to us through death, into eternal life—where God's final glory will be manifest.

7

THE BAPTISM OF THE LORD

The Watery Grave

I like doing baptisms. It is a very special event in the life of a family, always a happy occasion, usually without the drama that often surrounds weddings. However, sometimes I am the second priest the parents come to see about doing the ceremony. The first priest has given the parents a grilling: Are you going to return to the practice of the faith? Are you going to become registered and a paid-up member of the parish? Will you be sending the child to a Catholic school? Some parents are even told that *unless* you attend the parish's baptismal course or preparation evening then you *cannot* have your baby baptized. Nonsense!

While formation is desirable, even the Church's law states that Catholic parents have a right to have their children baptized if they reasonably ask for it, are properly disposed, are not prohibited from receiving this sacrament (because they have been baptized before, for example) and that there is a "realistic hope" that he or she will be brought up in the Catholic faith.

That some parents are not very articulate about why they want to have their baby baptized is insufficient grounds for them to be rejected. They may have a vague sense that it is a good idea, or be sincere in doing their best in raising the child Catholic, or doing it because Nana said we had to! Regardless, where you start the process does not matter; it is all about where God can finish it.

Sometimes, I am also the second priest a couple who wants to get married comes to see. The first priest has found out that they are living together and so gives them a hard time, saying, "Well, we cannot do your wedding until you stop living together, stop having sexual intercourse, and make a good confession." Some of those couples walk out of that parish office right into the arms of a civil marriage celebrant. Sometimes they come and see me.

I see these parents and couples because I live by a very easy principle: I baptize anything that moves; I marry anything that moves; and I bury anything that doesn't!

Don't tell some priests this, but they do not own the sacraments. Christ does. This is rock-solid Catholic sacramental theology. Christ baptizes, marries, confirms, forgives, ordains, anoints, and hosts us all at the Eucharist. I may be administering the sacrament in Christ's name, but Christ is the actor. Don't get me wrong, I believe in the good order of sacraments. I am not liturgically cavalier, but last time I checked the Gospels, Jesus was never stingy with his presence, but went after those who lived at the fringe of his society, drawing them into the life and mercy of God through an encounter with this presence. That's one of the things sacraments are, a direct encounter with the presence of Christ, who went to those who did not fit the neat religious categories of his day. If it was good enough for Jesus, it's good enough for me!

Because of the Baptism of the Lord, we are all baptized into the life of Christ, and there are three things I think we should celebrate in regard to this great feast.

Even though it is often our Catholic instinct to say that the Eucharist is our most important sacrament, it is in fact baptism. Done only once in a lifetime, baptism is the gate through which we are offered all other sacramental encounters with Christ, and it initiates us into the life of the church, for it is one Christ, one faith, and one baptism.

Baptism is also our most ecumenical sacrament. If you ever wanted to belong to the Orthodox, Episcopalian or Anglican, Lutheran, United and Uniting, Continuing Presbyterian, or Methodist churches, you will never be rebaptized, and even in the worst days of sectarianism, the Catholic Church never rebaptized anyone. We received other Christians into full communion with the Catholic Church. The only two mainstream Christian denominations who will rebaptize are the Baptists, because they do not hold to infant baptism. They dedicate children and argue that baptism should be an adult decision. The other group is the Pentecostal Christians, because they argue that only a full immersion baptism is valid.

It is true that the Greek word, *bapto*, or *baptizo*, means "to wash" or "to immerse," and so full immersion better represents what it intends, namely, representing Jesus' tomb. We now encourage full immersion of adults and children. In this context, we can see that the deeper the font and the fuller the immersion, the more easily everyone present understands the power of the symbols. That said, it is strange that groups who want to be so biblically literal about the amount of water used at baptism are not literal about the place of the water: the River Jordan. So volume matters, geography doesn't.

The third stunning element of baptism is related to the second: the action of plunging our adults and children into the watery tomb of the font three times. And as we do, we call on the Trinity to enable them die to sin, and rise to the freedom of Christ's life. Understandably, many people think that, because we call on the Trinity while we do the action with the water, the triple movement is all about the Father, Son, and Holy Spirit. In fact, the triple movement symbolizes the three days Jesus spent in the tomb.

We are the only world religion to believe that God took our flesh and died. For just as Jesus went down into the water and rose out of it into a fresh outpouring of the Father's love for him; and later, he goes down into the tomb of human death and the Father raises him to new life; so we go down into the watery grave so as to rise to a life of being both loved by God and being invited to live a life worthy of eternal life.

The first baptism at which I presided was for my niece Emily. I was fresh out of theological college and gung-ho for full immersion baptism. My uncle, who was a priest and my family's local pastor, had recently built a new parish church with a full-immersion font. My mother did not think it was a great idea. "Why would you distress that child so much with this unnecessary fuss? You always go overboard!" she said. That night, while doing some baptismal preparation at my brother and sister-in-law's home, I got the sense they did not think full immersion was necessary either, so I played dirty. "Peter," I said, "you have to know that Mother thinks full immersion is a terrible idea." "Good," he replied, "we'll do it then!"

On the day, at the big moment, I took Emily in my arms and said, "Emily Jane, I baptize you in the name of the Father" and lowered her in and out of the warm water. She thought it was a bath. "And of the Son," repeating the action. "And of the Holy Spirit," but this time I cupped my hand and gently poured some water over her head as well and with that, a little of the water went into her eye and she let out a huge scream. My mother jumped up from the first pew, "I told you this was a stupid idea." To which my brother sharply retorted, "Mum, will you please sit down and shut up." I tell that story to console you just in case you think you have a dysfunctional family. We have family fights at baptisms.

There are no half measures about immersion, we are in there boots and all. Because of the incarnation and the Lord's baptism by John at the Jordan, we don't have a detached God who only presides over us. We don't have a coaching God, who sits on the sidelines barking orders at us on the field of life. And we don't have a policeman God, who wants to catch us breaking the rules. We have a God who, in Jesus the Lord, immersed himself in our world, heart and mind, soul and divinity, boots and all.

For all those baptized in Christ, a curious thing happens. As Jesus fully immersed himself in our world, so we are fully immersed in Christ. But we are not spared from the world as if we are initiated into a reclusive religious sect. Just as Jesus' baptism was the beginning of his public ministry, so too, we are sent out to the world knowing that even though we sin, we are loved by a merciful God and are pleasing to him. We are sent out to immerse ourselves in the world and discover that Christ has gone ahead of us and dwells there too.

Welcomed and Saved; Called and Sent

Through Jesus' own baptism by John, we have a share in the dignity of baptism done in his name, which also proclaims, "Here is my son or daughter, and I love them."

Let's think about the baptism of our children, though much of what I will say applies to adults as well. Baptism recognizes that all of us are more than we can see and touch, that we have a creative and loving spirit or soul that equally defines who we are, and that this spiritual life within us shares in God and is God in us. We don't have to use any imagination to look in the face of our children and recognize that something greater is going on here than we can see. If we recognize this spiritual dimension in the lives of our children, then we have obligations to nurture it and not allow it to die in them.

What we do at baptisms is welcome children into a community that can provide them with a sense of belonging to a family of believers around the world, that has an ancient tradition of saints and sinners who have found within Christian faith a purpose, direction, and meaning for their lives. We are given the grace to stare down sin and destruction and to live a life worthy of being baptized in Christ. It enables us to deal with the ups and downs of our lives and to hold onto hope in this world, and in the life to come after death.

The entire rite of baptism underlines the dignity of the person being initiated into the life of Christ and as a member of the church. But why bother with being initiated into the church?

In an increasingly hostile world to religion, having and holding faith can be a very arduous business. We need each other and we are not meant to be soldiering on our own. There was a good reason why Jesus left behind a community. Christ was never under any illusions about what following his lead may cost, but he underlines how much we need each other to survive in this world. And we need his protection. We often like to feel so self-sufficient these days that we bristle when we hear how Christ "protects" us, but that is precisely what he does. And that protection comes through prayer, reading the Word, celebrating the Sacraments, and participating in the life of the Church.

When I do a baptism, I always start by saying that for the first 300 years of the Church's history, this sacrament was celebrated at dawn on the Easter Vigil, not only because the rising sun symbolized Christ's light dawning into our lives, but because baptism was always done in secret. For centuries, Christians who took the waters of baptism at dawn could be dead by lunchtime. For them, baptism was no social day out; it was a life and death commitment. Standing on the shoulders of the martyrs, most of us now gather for baptism in freedom and peace.

In the early church, there was not much preparation for the sacrament of baptism. In those days, anyone who professed the faith and was prepared to risk his or her life because of it was thought to be ready. A lengthy period of instruction in "the way" of the Christian life came immediately after baptism. The ancient rite of baptism is itself a teacher.

I always start the ceremony at the back door of the church, since this is the first formal time we will receive this child into the place where the church gathers. Using actions and words that extend back to the birth of our faith, and in some instances beyond it, we begin by asking the parents what name they have chosen for their child. I always look up the meaning of these names. It is often a revelation as to the child's personality.

Then the parents and sponsors declare that they understand what they are doing and are prepared to be Christian role models for this child. Then, as a way to confirm the declarations just made, the child is claimed for Christ by the sign of his cross.

Then we process to the font. I point out that this procession is not just about getting from point A to point B, but that it begins all the processions this child will make in his or her life into a church: for confirmation, Eucharist, penance, marriage, holy orders, and anointing of the sick. It also reminds us of that day when, please God, none of us will be around, but, at a big age and surrounded by their family and friends, they will recess out of the church for the final time in the rite of Christian burial.

After the readings and during the homily, I enjoy telling the godparents the history of their role. Most people like being a godfather or a godmother, but they haven't got a clue where the practice comes from. As noted earlier, the church no longer speaks about godfathers or godmothers. It speaks about sponsors, but, that term has not taken off in regard to infant baptism. Godparents remain in vogue.

Godparents come from the time when the earliest Christians could be martyred for the faith. Many of them had left their Jewish or Gentile families to join the Christian community, so if they were killed for the faith they did not want their children to return to their non-Christian extended families. In this context, they asked other Christians, in God's name, to swear they would take their children into their homes and raise them as their own, becoming their mother or father.

Given this history, we see why asking an atheist, agnostic, or a non-Christian to be a godparent does not make much sense. They may be terrific human beings, but effectively they have to say at the ceremony, "I will sponsor you into this church, and support you in it, but I have never joined it myself, or, I did join it and left years ago!"

These days, parents can make whatever arrangements they want about legal guardianship, but the role that a godparent can play in a child's life is, potentially, still very special. It is important that they take it seriously. At very least, I tell godparents never to forget the birthday of their godchild. I think we should be able to trade in any godparent who forgets our birthday on a new model. I also suggest that it would be good if godparents remember the date of the child's baptism, because this is the moment when they entered this child's life in the most special of ways. There is not a day between the time of baptism and the child's eighteenth birthday when the parents can say to a godfather or godmother, "Butt out, it's none of your business!" At baptism a godchild becomes a godparent's business, and we hope, on behalf of the entire Christian community, they will take their responsibilities very seriously indeed.

After the Liturgy of the Word, we remember that this child has patron saints who are praying with us right now in heaven, and we call on them by name. Rather than saying the names of a number of dead people who most people have never heard of, I do some research and give a very brief biography of the child's patron saints, who they are and why they are canonized. It brings the litany of the saints alive.

As soon as I say the word *exorcism*, I know that half the congregation is thinking of a 1973 film. We do not, however, think there is anything evil in this child. In the prayer of exorcism, we not only pray that the child be free of the common human condition expressed in and through original sin, but that, like Jesus at his baptism, they know an outpouring of God's love. I also hope and pray that this child will grow up to be protected from harm, recognize evil wherever it exists, and diminish evil's presence and power in the world. I do not know a believing parent who, these days, would not pray that their child would not be shielded by and enveloped in the love of God.

I remind the congregation that the anointing before baptism is done with the oil of catechumens—of those entering the church—and it is done on the breast bone. Early Christians, like all ancient peoples, believed that the heart was the place of love. It is with us to this day in the tradition of St. Valentine. In this anointing, we pray that the strength of Christ's power we seek may be found in this child having a heart of love for God, for their neighbor, and for themselves.

After blessing the water at the font, we profess our common Christian faith. I remind everyone that, in the early church, the commitment to baptism was so serious that just before the moment of baptism, it was as though the earliest Christians said, "Do you share our beliefs? Do you know what you are doing? Are you sure you wish to proceed?" This has come down to us as our profession of faith, and we proceed to a series of questions to which nearly every mainstream Christian can say yes. I must admit my favorite question is, "Do you reject Satan, all his works, and all his empty promises?" I love the idea of evil often offering us "empty promises." Perfect!

The anointing with chrism is done using the church's holiest oil, also used at the coronations of kings and queens, ordinations of priests and bishops, and at the sacrament of confirmation. In doing so, we welcome this girl or boy into the royal family of Christ, his school of prophets and the priesthood of all believers.

These days I ask the parents not to bring their children already dressed in their baptismal robe so that after baptism, and in line with the more ancient custom, we can vest them in their baptismal robe, as the physical reminder that they have just put on the life of Christ. We have these dramatic descriptions of baptisms at the Easter Vigil, where the candidates came in their work clothes, were smeared with oil, fully immersed in water, and then taken away, to soon return in the long white robe of baptism. This is where the white alb that the priest wears at Mass comes from. It is not a robe of the ordained; it is the white robe of the common priesthood of all Christ's faithful. Anyone who has been baptized could wear their white alb, or baptismal robe, to Mass.

We then present the parents and godparents with the light of Christ, for this child has been "enlightened by Christ" and is "always to walk as a child of the Light." Now, because we almost always get to keep our baptismal candle after the ceremony, it is wonderful to think it might be lit again at the other sacraments of initiation: Eucharist and confirmation. It also makes sense for that candle to be a light at their marriage or ordination ceremonies, and to be buried with them at the rite of burial as they go out to meet the Lord "with all the saints in the heavenly kingdom."

Finally, we pray that Christ will soon touch and open the child's eyes and ears to read and hear God's word, and their mouth to proclaim it to the glory of God.

The reason we have such an elaborate ritual is because of the baptism of the Lord. In it, and like the other Christ we are now meant to be, we discover that our true identity is in God, that we are beloved by him, and, through Christ, we have become members of God's family, his sons and daughters.

What more appropriate way of welcoming anyone into the world than having a community of frail, human believers initiate its members by reminding them that original sin does not have the last word, original grace does.

For those of us baptized in Christ, the Father's love and mercy always and everywhere has the final say on everything and everyone.

The task every day away from our baptism is to keep claiming our Christian dignity by how we choose to spend our lives, and to change our world for the better because of the love lavishly announced about us and to us at our baptisms.